MW01444858

H. P. LOVECRAFT
NIGHTMARE COUNTRIES

H. P. LOVECRAFT

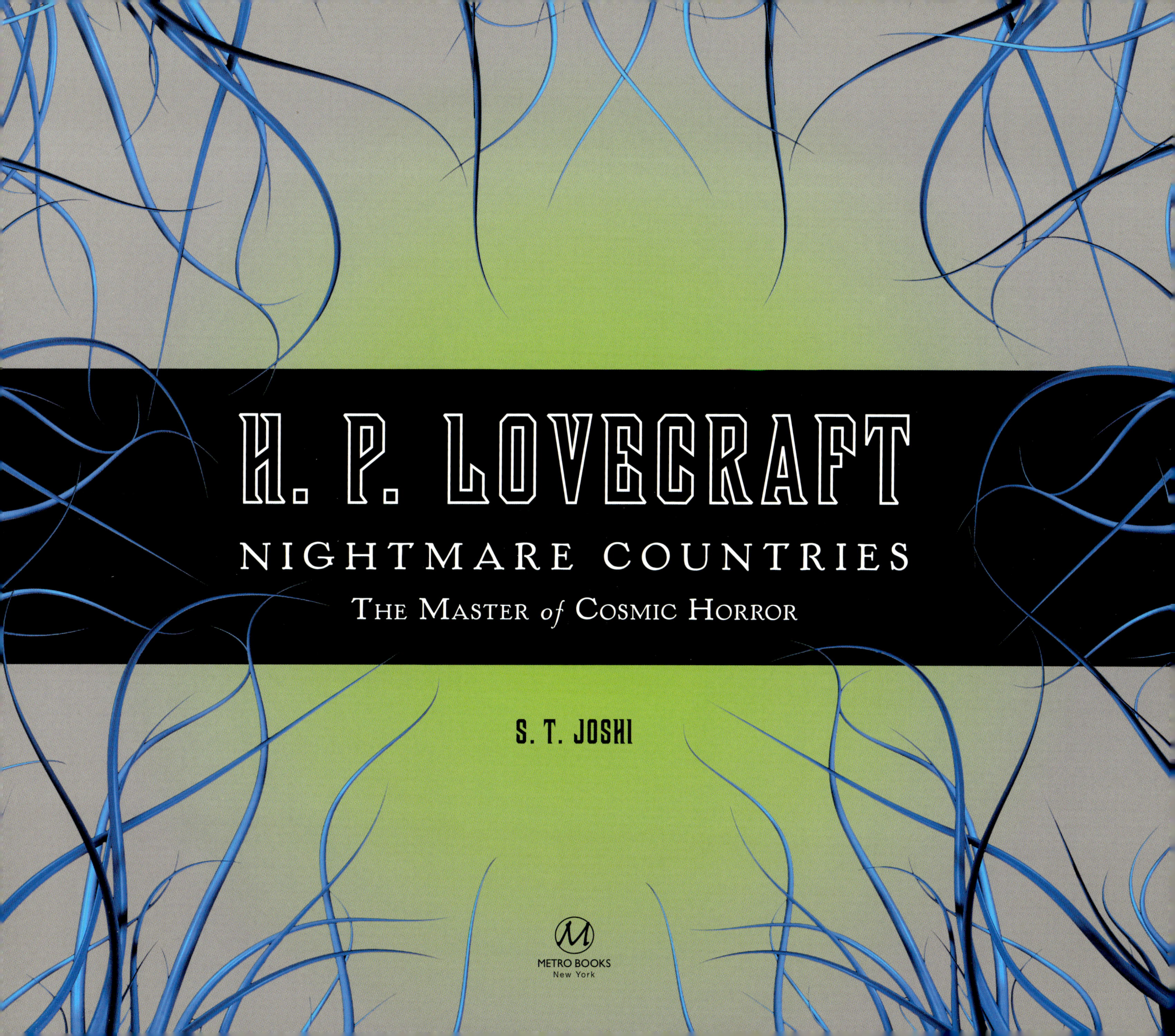

NIGHTMARE COUNTRIES
The Master of Cosmic Horror

S. T. JOSHI

METRO BOOKS
New York

METRO BOOKS
New York

An Imprint of Sterling Publishing
387 Park Avenue South
New York, NY 10016

METRO BOOKS and the distinctive Metro Books logo are trademarks of Sterling Publishing Co., Inc.

© 2012 by becker&mayer! LLC
Text © 2012 by S. T. Joshi

This 2012 edition published by Metro Books by arrangement with becker&mayer!

All rights reserved. No part of this publication may be reproduced, stored in a retrieval system, or transmitted, in any form or by any means, electronic, mechanical, photocopying, recording, or otherwise, without prior written permission from the publisher.

Designer: Rosebud Eustace
Editor: Kjersti Egerdahl
Photo Research: Amelia Boldaji and Katie del Rosario
Production Coordinator: Shirley Woo
Managing Editor: Michael del Rosario

ISBN 978-1-4351-4152-0

For information about custom editions, special sales, and premium and corporate purchases, please contact Sterling Special Sales at 800-805-5489 or specialsales@sterlingpublishing.com.

Manufactured in China

2 4 6 8 10 9 7 5 3 1
www.sterlingpublishing.com

CONTENTS

Introduction | 6

1
A Genuine Pagan (1890–1904) | 14

2
Eccentric Recluse (1904–1914) | 32

3
A Renewed Will to Live (1914–1924) | 50

4
New York Exile (1924–1926) | 78

5
The Creation of Cthulhu (1926–1931) | 94

6
A Shadow Over Life (1932–1937) | 120

7
The Mythos Grows | 142

Author Biography | 158

Image Credits | 160

INTRODUCTION

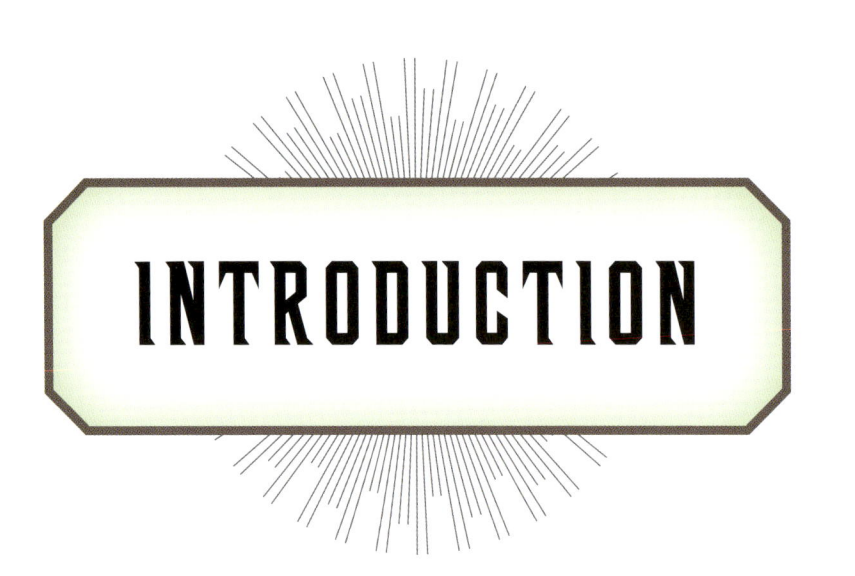

If H. P. Lovecraft were alive today, he would be astounded at the celebrity that he and his work have attained in the seventy-five years since his passing in 1937. Here was a man who had only one poorly printed book of his fiction published during his lifetime, and who was forced to publish most of his tales in *Weird Tales* and other pulp magazines of the 1920s and 1930s. Lovecraft was a virtual nonentity in the mainstream literary world of his day, and not a single article about him appeared in a major magazine or newspaper during his lifetime. He would have been forgiven for thinking, on his deathbed, that his work was destined to achieve the oblivion that he, in his excessive humility, believed it deserved.

Today, books of his stories, novelettes, and short novels have been printed in the millions of copies in hardcover and paperback, and have been translated into more than twenty-five languages around the world. Virtually every scrap of his writing—essays, poetry, and especially his thousands of surviving letters—has been published or is in the process of being published. The Cthulhu Mythos—the pseudomythological framework that he devised in his final decade—has taken on a life of its own, and hundreds of writers have contributed to it.

Lovecraft's presence is also felt in a variety of media. Radio adaptations of his tales began in the 1940s, film and television adaptations in the 1960s, and in 1982 a popular role-playing game achieved wide popularity, creating thousands of Lovecraft fans among those who had never read a word of his fiction. Lovecraft-related merchandise has taken off in the past couple of decades, ranging from such flippancies as "Cthulhu for President" bumper stickers to plush dolls in the shape of the octopoid extraterrestrial entity Cthulhu.

Most surprising of all, the very image of the gaunt, lantern-jawed, and self-effacing author has become an icon in popular culture, with many novels and comics using Lovecraft as a character, sometimes paired up with such fictional figures as Sherlock Holmes and at other times engaging in supernatural quests more bizarre than anything depicted in his own fiction. The teetotaling author from Providence, Rhode Island, would be mortified to know that a specialty beer has been named after him, and that a horror-themed bar called The Lovecraft has opened in Portland, Oregon.

How did this humble New Englander, perennially plagued with doubts about the merits of his own writing and resolutely determined to pursue literature as "self-expression" without any thought of sales or marketing, become such a popular and critically acclaimed figure? It is the task of this book to provide at least some partial answers to what may be an unanswerable conundrum, by examining the significant events of Lovecraft's life, the essence of his literary work, and the tremendous posthumous success that he has enjoyed.

ABOVE: *H. P. Lovecraft in 1934. One of several photos taken by Lucius B. Truesdell when Lovecraft was visiting his young friend R. H. Barlow in Florida.*

INTRODUCTION

7

ABOVE: *Edgar Allan Poe, the leading literary influence on Lovecraft's work.*

Lovecraft's life, like that of many authors, is perhaps lacking in noteworthy events but is full of interesting details. His development as a writer and thinker over a very short period–little more than two decades–is remarkable. No one who had read his early tales of horror and the macabre could have guessed that he would become the most significant writer of supernatural fiction in the twentieth century, rivaling only his fellow countryman Edgar Allan Poe as the supreme figure in this curious literary genre.

The documentary evidence on Lovecraft's life and work is almost inexhaustibly rich. In the course of his short life, he wrote as many as eighty thousand letters, becoming one of the most prolific letter writers in human history. Only about five thousand of these letters now survive, but many of them are highly revealing of his tastes and temperament; some of them extend to forty, fifty, even seventy pages, longer than most of his tales. As such, Lovecraft has become one of the most self-documented figures of his age, and there are periods in his life when we can obtain an almost daily chronicle of his activities.

What is more, many of his friends and colleagues have written memoirs about Lovecraft, adding fascinating details beyond what he himself discusses in his letters. A few of these memoirs are of book length and provide illuminating accounts of a man who left a strong impression on all those with whom he came into contact, even those who knew him only by correspondence.

One must, of course, exercise caution in evaluating this wealth of documentary evidence, whether it comes from Lovecraft's own pen or from that of others. On occasion it can seem as if Lovecraft, in his letters, is presenting a carefully fashioned image of himself—he liked to pose, even in his twenties, as a preternaturally aged gentleman, devoted to the past and scorning all the social, political, and cultural movements of his own day. But on the whole, his letters seem quite candid about both the ups and downs of his life, and his friends' memoirs only augment, and do not contradict, the image that emerges from Lovecraft's own letters and essays.

The literary genre that Lovecraft revolutionized in his short career was one that he himself called "weird fiction." The literature of supernatural horror has a very long pedigree, and its origins can be traced to the earliest surviving writings of Western civilization. The *Epic of Gilgamesh*, a fragmentary Babylonian poem dating to about 1700 BC, already introduces such motifs as the superhero, the quest for eternal life, and a descent into the underworld. Homer's *Odyssey* (c. 700 BC) is full of supernatural creatures of all sorts, from the sorceress Circe (who can turn human beings into beasts) to the lumbering one-eyed Cyclops. Greek tragedy is peppered with ghosts, magic potions, and other wondrous phenomena. The first known werewolf in literature is found in a brief passage in Petronius's *Satyricon* (c. AD 65).

With the dawn of the Christian era, such figures as the witch, the ghost, and the vampire took on new significance, since they were all tied to various phases of Christian theology, particularly in the influence of Satan upon a fallen humanity. The grotesque images of Hell in Dante's *Inferno* (c. 1314) and the vivid descriptions of Satan and his minions in John Milton's *Paradise Lost* (1667) are perhaps too closely tied to religion to constitute weird literature in their own right, but they both exercised considerable influence on what came after.

In order for a true literature of the *supernatural* to emerge, there needs to be a general consensus on what constitutes the *natural*. In other words, human knowledge must have advanced to the point where there is widespread consensus that such creatures as witches, vampires, and werewolves *cannot* exist because they defy what have come to be known as the natural laws governing the universe. As Lovecraft himself stated in a letter, "The crux of a weird tale is something which *could not possibly happen.*" It is therefore not surprising that supernatural horror as a literary genre did not arise until the late eighteenth century, for only then had science developed a reasonably firm understanding of natural law; only then did tales of supernatural horror become sufficiently separated from myth, folklore, and religion.

The short novel *The Castle of Otranto* (1764), written by a dilettantish English nobleman, Horace Walpole, exercised an influence far beyond its actual merits, for it launched the so-called Gothic novel that dominated literary history for the next half century or more. Walpole's little book, full of outlandish and preposterous incidents, set the basic parameters of the Gothic novel: the medieval setting (it was believed that the ignorance and barbarism of that era provided fertile ground for belief in the supernatural); the use of the castle as a stage setting (later adapted as the motif of the haunted house); and the use of stock characters, such as the ruthless nobleman, the beautiful young woman as potential victim, and the courageous young man who saves the day.

More than four hundred Gothic novels were published during the period 1764–1824, but only a few of these are of interest today; the great majority of them were written by hacks who sought to capitalize on the popularity of the genre. One of the most significant Gothic novelists was Ann Radcliffe, who in *The Mysteries of Udolpho* (1794) and other works pioneered the technique of the "explained supernatural," in which seemingly supernatural incidents were explained away as the result of error or trickery. Although this deflation of the supernatural can often seem anticlimactic, Radcliffe achieved tremendous popularity.

Matthew Gregory Lewis, in *The Monk* (1796), and Charles Robert Maturin, in *Melmoth the Wanderer* (1820), used the supernatural unabashedly. Both books, widely regarded as pinnacles of Gothic writing, involve pacts with the devil that go hideously astray. It was during this period that Mary Shelley wrote *Frankenstein* (1818), a remarkably advanced work that some believe to be the first work of science fiction.

It was, however, Edgar Allan Poe, in the 1830s and 1840s, who transformed the dying Gothic tradition into

ABOVE: *Dr. Frankenstein beholds his creation in an illustration by Theodor M. von Holst.*

I started from my sleep with horror; a cold dew covered my forehead, my teeth chattered, and every limb became convulsed; when, by the dim and yellow light of the moon, as it forced its way through the window shutters, I beheld the wretch— the miserable monster whom I had created. He held up the curtain of the bed; and his eyes, if eyes they may be called, were fixed on me. His jaws opened, and he muttered some inarticulate sounds, while a grin wrinkled his cheeks.

~FRANKENSTEIN, MARY SHELLEY

something of far greater aesthetic worth. With an unparalleled understanding of the psychology of fear, and with a prose style of grim intensity, Poe virtually invented the short story as we know it and produced, in his tragically brief career, a body of horror fiction that remains unparalleled in its scope and quality.

Poe's work spans the spectrum of the weird. There are tales of supernatural horror such as the celebrated "The Fall of the House of Usher," where Roderick Usher, his sister Madeline, and the house itself share a single soul and suffer a joint dissolution, and "Ligeia," where a dead first wife's will to live is so strong that it recasts the face of a second wife. Poe excelled in psychological horror, such as "The Pit and the Pendulum," with its memorable depiction of the tortures of the Spanish Inquisition. He also wrote tales of ambiguous supernaturalism: for example, in "The Tell-Tale Heart," we do not know whether the murdered man's heart is actually beating under the floorboards, or whether the murderer is merely conjuring up the sound in his own mind.

In England, during the later nineteenth century, a great many writers tried their hand at the supernatural, especially in that form of the supernatural known as the ghost story. Charles Dickens, in *A Christmas Carol* (1843), used the ghost story somewhat heavy-handedly to point a moral. The Irishman Joseph Sheridan Le Fanu, in "Green Tea" (1869), produced a chilling tale of a clergyman beset by a supernatural monkey. Le Fanu also wrote a striking tale of a lesbian vampire, "Carmilla" (1871), which set the stage for Bram Stoker's *Dracula* (1897). Stoker's novel, of course, became the prototypical account of the care and feeding of vampires. Robert Louis Stevenson, in *The Strange Case of Dr. Jekyll and Mr. Hyde* (1886), and Oscar Wilde, in *The Picture of Dorian Gray* (1891), wrote tales of a doppelgänger, or double. In America, the cynical journalist Ambrose Bierce became Poe's greatest successor in the imperishable tales of supernatural and psychological horror he wrote in *Tales of Soldiers and Civilians* (1891) and *Can Such Things Be?* (1893).

At the turn of the century, four supreme masters of weird fiction emerged, showing that the genre had reached a pinnacle of literary polish and sophistication.

The Welshman Arthur Machen, in *The Great God Pan* (1894) and other works, postulated the existence of a hideous race of stunted half-human creatures, the Little People, who lurked on the underside of civilization. Machen, a fervent Anglo-Catholic who felt that the advance of science was robbing the world of its stores of mystery and wonder, infused his tales with a *conviction* that few others could match. Lovecraft believed that his novella "The White People" (1904), a mesmerizing tale of a teenage girl who, without her knowledge, is inculcated into the witch cult by her evil nurse, was one of the towering achievements of weird literature.

The Irishman Lord Dunsany wrote *The Gods of Pegāna* (1905) and other works of imaginary-world fantasy, anticipating the later work of J. R. R. Tolkien. Dunsany evolved a prose style, based partially on the King James Bible, of unmatched fluency and evocativeness. In his earliest books he fashioned an entire cosmogony of imagined gods, demigods, and worshippers—an achievement from which Lovecraft took inspiration when he came to devise his own pseudomythology.

M. R. James, a distinguished English academic, wrote four immensely influential collections of ghost stories that raised that subgenre to its highest levels of artistry. James was a master of story construction, and the complex structure of his tales was highly suggestive to Lovecraft when he came to write the longer narratives of his final decade. Lovecraft later admitted, however, that James was the "earthiest member of the 'big four'" because of the relatively conventional nature of his weird phenomena.

In Lovecraft's opinion, Algernon Blackwood's 1907 story "The Willows" was the best weird tale ever written—a haunting tale of nebulous horrors encountered by two men floating on a raft down the Danube. In novels and tales alike, Blackwood expressed a mystical vision that wavered between horror and awe. In his best work, such as the story collection *Incredible Adventures* (1914), awe is dominant, and the supernatural phenomena evoke the kind of transcendent emotion we associate with religion.

The literature of the supernatural was, at the time of Lovecraft's birth, a rich and diverse genre, but it was still regarded as something of a curiosity in the general literary world; many readers and critics did not believe it was an entirely legitimate literary form, and it was scorned as offering empty escapism from the harsh realities of life. In the course of his life, Lovecraft perennially sought to find the greatest works of weird fiction for his personal enjoyment, but as his career progressed, he himself became the most revolutionary figure in the field since Poe.

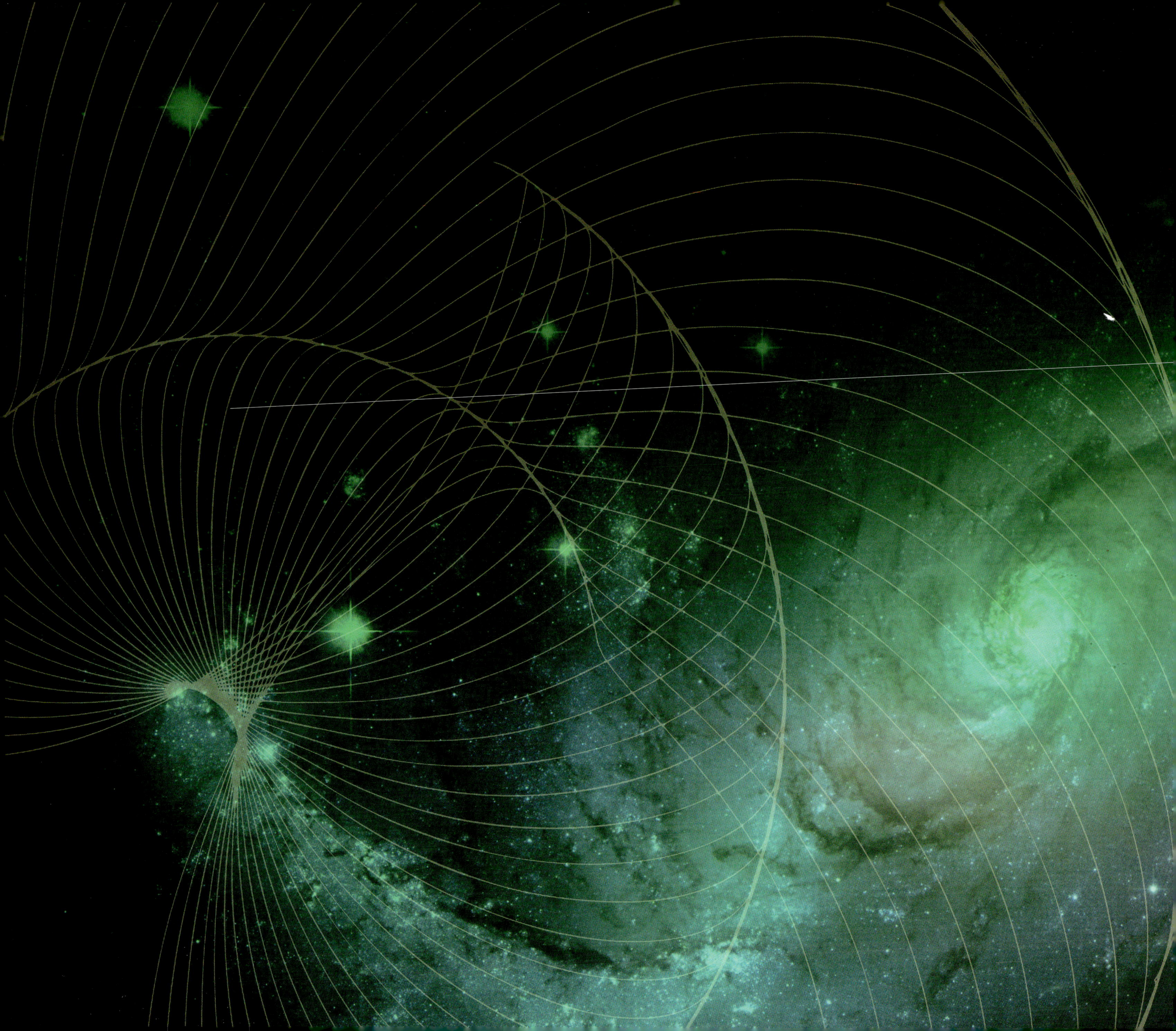

I

A GENUINE PAGAN

(1890–1904)

There are numerous questions and ambiguities about Lovecraft's ancestry, parentage, and early life, and many of these probably cannot be resolved. Lovecraft himself believed that his paternal ancestry dated to fifteenth-century England; but, although the names Lovecraft or Lovecroft can be found that early, Lovecraft's own direct lineage cannot be traced earlier than Joseph Lovecraft (1775–1850), his great-grandfather. This man relocated his family from his home in Devon to the United States, settling in Rochester, New York, around 1830. Lovecraft's father, Winfield Scott Lovecraft, was born in 1853 and, as a teenager, worked for a time as a blacksmith's apprentice.

Lovecraft's maternal ancestors, the Phillipses, are a much more distinguished line, extending back to at least the late seventeenth century. The family settled in the area around Foster, a small town in western Rhode Island, where Lovecraft's grandfather, Whipple Van Buren Phillips, was born in 1833. He made his fortune in a variety of business ventures and married Roby Alzada Place Phillips. Sarah Susan Phillips (b. 1857), Lovecraft's mother, was Whipple's and Roby's second child. In his later life Lovecraft had close relationships with his two aunts,

ABOVE: *Lovecraft's birthplace, 454 Angell Street, Providence.*

Lillian (b. 1856) and Annie (b. 1866), but never had much to do with his uncle, Edwin (b. 1864).

How Lovecraft's parents ever could have met is a mystery. Winfield was employed by Gorham Silversmiths, a prominent company in Providence. He was a "commercial traveler"—not a traveling salesman as such (he did not solicit

H. P. LOVECRAFT

> "I CAN SEE MYSELF AS A CHILD . . . FEELING THE IMMINENCE OF SOME WONDER WHICH I COULD NEITHER DESCRIBE NOR FULLY CONCEIVE."
>
> —H. P. Lovecraft

door-to-door), but one who sold to wholesalers. Nevertheless, his social standing was significantly lower than that of Sarah Susan ("Susie") Phillips, who was part of the informal Providence aristocracy. One conjures up the image of the couple meeting secretly in out-of-the-way places to escape the wrath of Whipple Phillips. The reality was probably not quite as dramatic as this, and it is possible that Whipple himself, in the course of his business dealings, made Winfield's acquaintance in the hope that he might prove to be a suitable husband for one of his three daughters, all of whom were still single into their late twenties. The couple married in Boston on June 12, 1889, and settled in Dorchester, a suburb of Boston, where they planned to build a home. Just over a year later, on August 20, 1890, their only son, Howard Phillips Lovecraft, was born. Susie had gone back to the family home at 454 Angell Street to have the baby, but after a few months she returned to her husband in Dorchester.

For the next several years, the couple lived in various Boston suburbs. In the winter of 1892–93 the Lovecrafts apparently stayed in Auburndale with the young poet and essayist Louise Imogen Guiney and her mother. For the rest of his life Lovecraft recalled the magical vista of standing on a railway bridge in Auburndale at sunset, "feeling

A GENUINE PAGAN

the imminence of some wonder which I could neither describe nor fully conceive." This may have been the first time he felt that sense of the cosmic that would infuse so much of his fiction.

A precocious boy, Lovecraft was a rapid talker at the age of two and could recite Mother Goose poems from the tabletop. Guiney, as a poet, encouraged his devotion to meter. Because of the boy's long, golden hair (which turned brown in adulthood) and cheerful disposition, she nicknamed him "Little Sunshine." He was also dandled on the knee of the venerable literary figure Oliver Wendell Holmes, who was a friend of Guiney's.

Susie Lovecraft seems to have had mixed feelings about her own son. She had hoped for a daughter and had begun a hope chest for her. When Howard was born, she dressed him in frocks for years, far beyond what was normal at the time. Indeed, his aunt Annie once mentioned that Lovecraft, as a very small boy, would sometimes say "I'm a little girl!" Susie also liked Lovecraft's long hair—and she cried when, at the age of six, he made her cut off his curls.

Lovecraft's idyllic childhood came to an abrupt and tragic end in April 1893 when Winfield, on a business trip in Chicago, suffered some kind of attack or seizure. He was

ABOVE: *Oliver Wendell Holmes, a leading literary figure of the nineteenth century, whom Lovecraft met as a child.*

RIGHT: *Lovecraft's drawing of his family's coat of arms. The motto, "Quae Amamus Tuemur," means "We defend the things we love."*

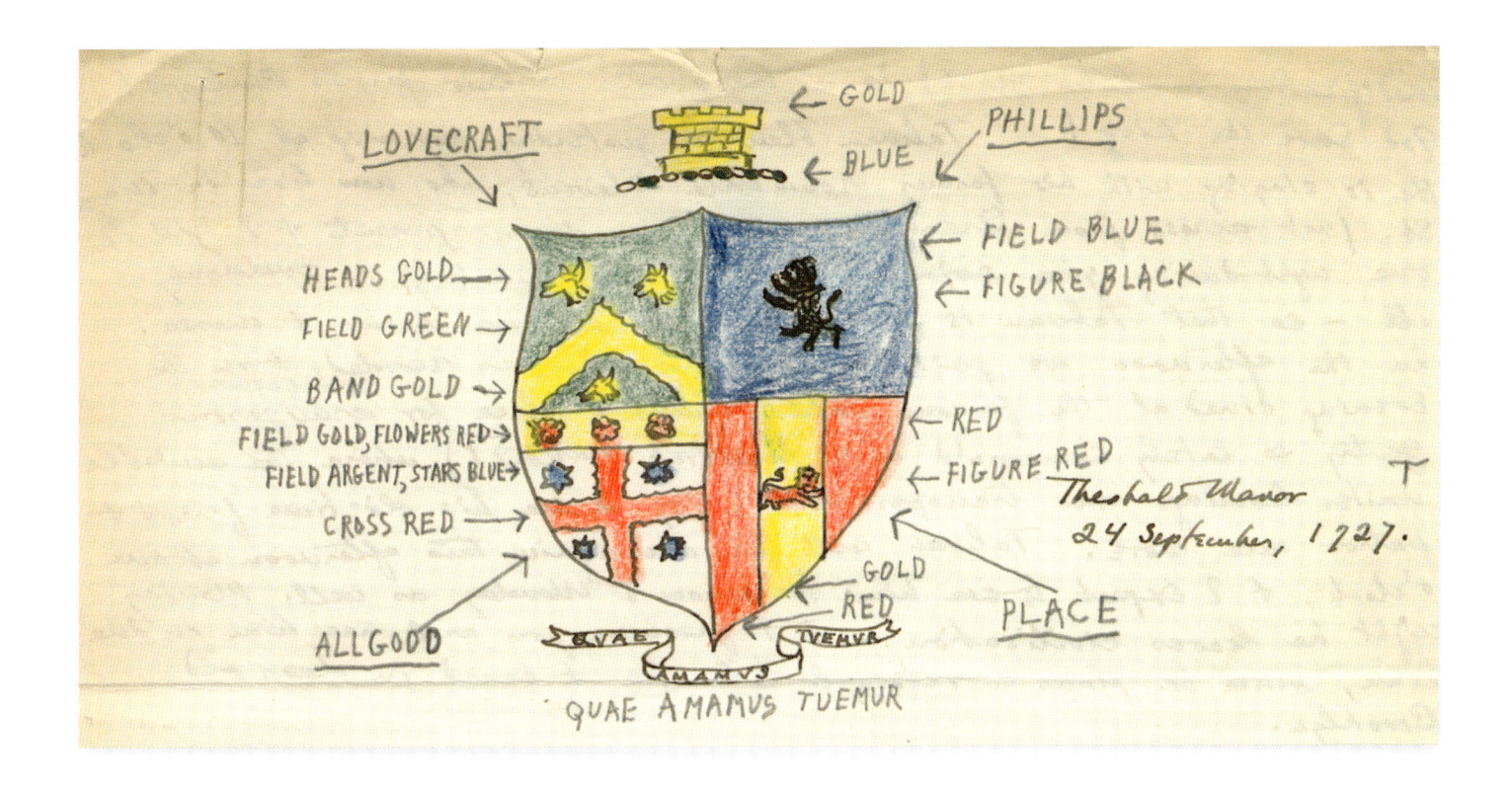

brought back under restraint and placed in Butler Hospital, a hospital for the insane on the East Side of Providence.

It is now clear that Winfield was suffering from syphilis. In all likelihood, he had contracted it from a prostitute in his late twenties, long before he and Susie were married. The treatment of syphilis at that period was at a very primitive stage (the spirochete that causes it was not identified until 1911), so Winfield was simply placed in the hospital as if he were an insane person and given virtually no medication. His condition deteriorated over the years, and he died on July 19, 1898. It is unclear what Lovecraft was told about his father's illness; in later years he claimed that Winfield was "seized with a complete paralytic stroke . . . [and was never afterward conscious," but this is clearly erroneous. It is probable that the boy was told this as an excuse for not visiting his father in the hospital, or he may have misconstrued the technical designation of Winfield's illness ("general paresis" or "general paralysis"). There is no evidence that either Howard or Susie ever saw Winfield at Butler Hospital.

This whole series of events must have been traumatic for Lovecraft and, especially, for his mother. They

A GENUINE PAGAN

19

ABOVE: *Whipple Van Buren Phillips, Lovecraft's maternal grandfather.*

promptly returned to the family home at 454 Angell Street, where Lovecraft grew up devoted to the city of his birth, Providence, and to his native state of Rhode Island.

Lovecraft was thrilled with the city's long and rich history, dating to 1636, especially in its colonial period. He loved its wide array of colonial houses and public buildings, particularly in the historic East Side, bounded on the west by the Providence River and on the east by the Seekonk River. This was also the location of College Hill, on top of which sits Brown University, founded in 1764 as King's College in the town of Warren, but moved to Providence in 1770. The East Side still boasts numerous large and distinguished homes built in the course of the nineteenth century as the town's citizens continued to prosper.

In the short term, the boy's upbringing fell to his mother, his aunts Lillian and Annie (who was now married to the journalist Edward F. Gamwell), and especially to his grandfather Whipple Phillips, a successful businessman who was involved in a number of different enterprises. These ranged from real estate speculation (he virtually established the small town of Greene, in western Rhode Island) to manufacturing to land development in the far West. It was he who had caused the large and lavishly furnished house at

ABOVE: *A 1907 Edmund Dulac illustration from the* Arabian Nights. *The book was one of Lovecraft's earliest introductions to the literature of fantasy.*

Presently we saw in the far distance what seemed to us to be a splendid palace, towards which we turned our weary steps, but when we reached it we saw that it was a castle, lofty, and strongly built. Pushing back the heavy ebony doors we entered the courtyard, but upon the threshold of the great hall beyond it we paused, frozen with horror, at the sight which greeted us. On one side lay a huge pile of bones—human bones, and on the other numberless spits for roasting!

–THE ARABIAN NIGHTS

454 Angell Street to be built in 1880–81, with space for five live-in servants. The house and grounds became a spacious area for the expansion of the boy's imagination and intellect. The house was then at the very edge of the developed part of the city, making Lovecraft feel simultaneously a part of the urban and the rural milieu. Whipple, for his part, showed his grandson objects from ancient Rome that he had brought back from his travels abroad, and he also told the boy extemporaneous weird tales, their imagery chiefly drawn from the old Gothic novels.

Lovecraft continued to reveal his precocity by reading at an early age—first *Grimms' Fairy Tales* at the age of four, then the *Arabian Nights* at five. He asked the family lawyer, Albert A. Baker, what a typical Arab name might be, and Baker devised the name Abdul Alhazred. It stuck with the child, and years later Lovecraft used the name for the author of the dreaded *Necronomicon*. Not long afterward, Lovecraft discovered the worlds of ancient Greece and Rome, initially through the charming retellings of myths found in Thomas Bulfinch's *The Age of Fable* (1855), then through actual translations of classical works found in the family library. Lovecraft gravitated to the old, eighteenth-century books that had been banished to the attic, and in this way he also developed a love of eighteenth-century poetry and prose that never left him. Indeed, he shocked his Yankee family by declaring himself, at the age of six, a loyal subject of Queen Victoria, not of President Grover Cleveland. He claimed that his devotion to England derived in part from the English ancestry of his father, and he exhibited this devotion in often contrarian ways. Throughout his life he used British spelling variants, and he even half-seriously regretted the "tragedy" of the American Revolution, wishing that the colonies had remained loyal to Great Britain.

It was around this time that the boy began his first attempts at writing—fiction, poetry, and scientific work. Poetry may have come first, as Lovecraft declares that his earliest poems dated to the age of six. The earliest surviving specimen, "The Poem of Ulysses," dates to 1897. It is a retelling of the *Odyssey* in the space of eighty-eight lines, with surprisingly sophisticated internal rhymes and meter. Here are the first four lines:

> The night was darke! O readers, Hark!
> And see Ulysses' fleet!
> From trumpets sound back homeward bound
> He hopes his spouse to greet.

But ancient Rome exercised an even greater fascination than Greek myth or literature, and around 1900 Lovecraft produced a remarkable item called "Ovid's *Metamorphoses*." This is a literal translation, in rhyming verse, of the first eighty-eight lines of Ovid's epic poem the *Metamorphoses*. Lovecraft had begun to learn Latin on his own at the age of eight, assisted by his grandfather; even so, it is remarkable that he could have produced such a competent translation at such an early age.

In 1902 he wrote his most polished early verse, *Poemata Minora*, Volume II (Volume I, written in 1901, does not survive). This small collection of five poems speaks poignantly of Lovecraft's devotion to the classical world and to the past in general. In later years he was fond of quoting the final stanza of "Ode to Selene or Diana":

> Take heed, *Diana*, of my humble plea.
> Convey me where my happiness may last.
> Draw me against the tide of time's rough sea
> And let my spirit dwell amid the past.

In comparison to his poetry, Lovecraft's early story writing is disappointingly crude. His earliest (non-surviving) specimen, "The Noble Eavesdropper," dates to 1897, and over the next few years he appears to have written a

ABOVE: *Queen Victoria, ruler of Great Britain, died in 1901 when Lovecraft was ten; a few years earlier the young Lovecraft announced to his family that he was her loyal subject, not President Grover Cleveland's.*

A GENUINE PAGAN

number of short stories, a few of which were preserved by his mother. One would have thought that Lovecraft's early readings of Grimms' fairy tales and the *Arabian Nights*, along with his rapturous discovery at the age of six of an edition of Samuel Taylor Coleridge's great horror poem *The Rime of the Ancient Mariner*, illustrated by Gustave Doré, would have led him to write supernatural tales, but such is not the case. Even his ecstatic reading of Poe at the age of eight did not lead immediately to the writing of Poe pastiches. Instead, what we have are comic tales of the sea ("The Little Glass Bottle"); a curiously gruesome tale of a small boy and his sister exploring an underground passageway ("The Secret Cave"); and, perhaps most interesting of all, "The Mystery of the Grave-yard; or, 'A Dead Man's Revenge.'"

This last story is inspired, not by Coleridge or Poe, but by dime novels. Dime novels were short paperback books that began to be published as early as 1860. They were generally regarded as crude popular literature, full of hair-raising adventures, recurring detective characters, and fast-paced, easy-reading prose. Dime novels generally appealed to young adults or the poor and ill-educated; they were generally condemned or ignored by highbrow critics, and Lovecraft himself in later years found it embarrassing that he had been so fond of them in his youth. His story "The Mystery of the Grave-yard" clearly follows the dime-novel formula in its creation of a detective, King John, who appeared in several other stories that do not survive.

Another important early intellectual influence was science. At the age of eight Lovecraft became fascinated by the science of chemistry, and shortly thereafter his mother gave him a chemistry set. He began writing almost immediately. On March 4, 1899, the first issue of his homemade paper, the *Scientific Gazette*, appeared; one passage reads: "There was a great explosion in the Providence Laboratory this afternoon. While experimenting some potassium blew up causing great damage to everyone." A total of thirty-two issues of the *Scientific Gazette* survive, the last dating to as late as 1909. This journal, like many others that Lovecraft wrote at this time, was reproduced by hectograph, an early kind of duplicating method that could generate up to fifty copies. Different colors could even be used. Most of the papers were handwritten, with Lovecraft neatly laying out the copy in columns in imitation of a newspaper. The mere fact that he used the hectograph must mean that his writings were popular among both his family and his growing band of young friends.

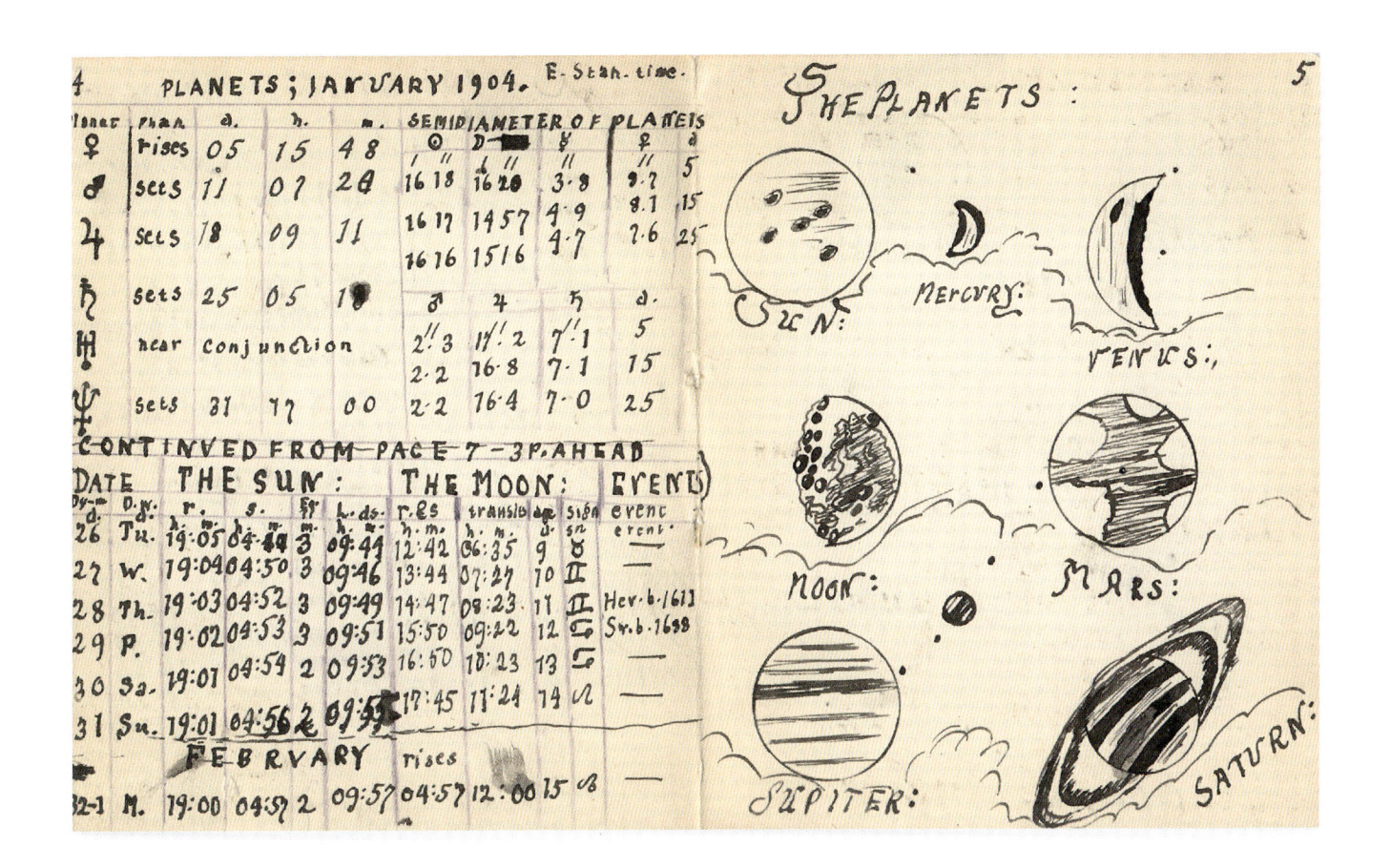

Amusingly, his interest in science led to Lovecraft's early discovery of the "facts of life." Looking through various manuals of anatomy at the age of eight, he learned all about the process of human reproduction and, by his own testimony, thereby lost all interest in the subject. "The whole matter was reduced to prosaic mechanism... and all the drama was taken out of it." In later years, Lovecraft revealed himself to be one of the most asexual of beings.

His discovery of chemistry paled in comparison to the rapture he felt on discovering astronomy. In early 1902, at the age of eleven, he found some old astronomy books that had been owned by his grandmother, and in this way he "discovered the myriad suns and worlds of infinite space."

ABOVE: *A page from the January 1904 issue of the* R.I. Journal of Science and Astronomy, *one of Lovecraft's juvenile periodicals.*

A GENUINE PAGAN

I began to have nightmares of the most hideous description, peopled with things which I called "night-gaunts"— a compound word of my own coinage. I used to draw them after waking (perhaps the idea of these figures came from an edition de luxe of *Paradise Lost* with illustrations by Doré, which I discovered one day in the east parlour).

–H. P. LOVECRAFT, LETTER TO RHEINHART KLEINER, 16 NOVEMBER 1916

ABOVE: *One of Gustave Doré's illustrations for John Milton's* Paradise Lost, *which might have influenced Lovecraft's dreams of "night-gaunts."*

He began collecting more up-to-date astronomy volumes and also did extensive writing on the subject. His most significant work was a weekly periodical, the *Rhode Island Journal of Astronomy*, which began in 1903 and of which sixty-nine issues, up to 1909, survive.

Lovecraft also wrote many separate treatises on astronomical subjects, including a nine-volume *Science Library* (dealing with such issues as telescopes, Galileo, and the moon), three of which survive in manuscript. He collected astronomical equipment, including several telescopes, the latest of which (a Bardon 3" from Montgomery Ward) cost a whopping $50.00.

It is clear that Lovecraft was a self-motivated learner; but what of formal schooling? At a time before school attendance was mandatory, Lovecraft's family made the decision to keep him out of elementary school until 1898. He had exhibited certain nervous disturbances as a very young child, and the trauma of his father's illness and death—whatever he may have known about it—could not have helped. The death, on January 26, 1896, of Lovecraft's grandmother was another disturbing event: the household was plunged in gloom, and the boy was so frightened at the black clothing worn by the female members of his family for months thereafter that he would surreptitiously pin bits of bright cloth or paper on their clothes for relief.

It was at this time that Lovecraft experienced horrible nightmares in which bizarre creatures that he called "night-gaunts" would plague him. He described these creatures as "black, lean, rubbery things with bared, barbed tails, bat-wings, and *no faces at all*." They would clutch him by the stomach and carry him off on nameless voyages, and the boy would frequently wake up screaming. Dreams and nightmares of this sort, some of them highly detailed and full of bizarre imagery, afflicted Lovecraft throughout his life, and several of them served as the basis of his weird tales.

Given his various nervous troubles, the family was perhaps uncertain of the effect of formal schooling on his temperament. Nevertheless, he was enrolled in the Slater Avenue School for the 1898–99 term. We know little of what he did during this year, and he was withdrawn after its conclusion and was not re-enrolled until the 1902–03 term. Back in school, Lovecraft finally began developing friendships with boys his own age. Among the closest of them were two brothers, Chester and Harold Munroe,

ABOVE: A Vanity Fair *illustration of one of young Lovecraft's favorite fictional characters, Sherlock Holmes, as portrayed by actor William Gillette circa 1900.*

who lived about four blocks away; Chester was a year older, Harold a year younger than Lovecraft.

One of their favorite activities was the Providence Detective Agency, where they played at being the successors to Sherlock Holmes. As Lovecraft wrote later in a letter: "Our force had very rigid regulations and carried in its pockets a standard working equipment of police whistle, magnifying glass, electric flashlight, handcuffs . . . tin badge, (I have mine still!!), tape measure (for footprints), revolver, (mine was the real thing, but Inspector Munroe . . . had a water squirt-pistol while Inspector [Ronald Upham . . . worried along with a cap-pistol) and copies of all newspaper accounts of desperate criminals at large . . ." It is rather disturbing to think of Lovecraft carrying an actual revolver with him, but we can hope it was not loaded.

Music was also an interest for the boys. Lovecraft had previously taken violin lessons for two years, but his mother ended them abruptly when he exhibited nervous strain from practicing; in later years he professed a profound lack of interest in classical music. But now, at the age of eleven, Lovecraft and his gang formed the Blackstone Military Band, and Lovecraft played an instrument called the zobo. He describes it as "a brass horn with a membrane at one end, which would transform humming to a delightfully brassy impressiveness." This sounds like a combination of a kazoo and a harmonica. He and his friends were captivated by the popular songs of the day, and years later he could still remember the lyrics to such tunes as "Bedelia" and "On the Banks of the Wabash."

It is refreshing to see Lovecraft behaving like a "normal" boy in his interactions with his friends, but his intellectual brilliance, his nervous troubles, and the coddling that his mother inflicted upon him probably made him more solitary than other boys. A neighbor, Clara Hess, tells a poignant story about his devotion to astronomy:

> Howard used to go out into the fields in back of my home to study the stars. One early fall evening several of the children in the vicinity assembled to watch him from a distance. Feeling sorry for his loneliness I went up to him and asked him about his telescope and was permitted to look through it. But his language was so technical that I could not understand it and I returned to my group and left him to his lonely study of the heavens.

In the summer of 1903 Lovecraft attended the graduation ceremonies at the Slater Avenue School, even though he had attended only for two years. He was, in fact, the class valedictorian, and he gave an extemporaneous speech about Sir William Herschel, a celebrated British astronomer. In 1903–04 he had private tutors. In a later letter he referred to one of them as "my odd, shy private tutor Arthur P. May–a theological student whom I loved to shock with my pagan materialism."

That last remark refers to the fact that Lovecraft had, by this time, apparently become a full-fledged atheist. As early as the age of five, he enrolled in a Sunday school, probably at the First Baptist Church, since most of his family were Baptists. He made such a nuisance of himself that he was allowed to drop out. Lovecraft's devotion to classical Greece and Rome, and his early scientific interests, appear to have led him to shed whatever religious beliefs he may have had. Indeed, he claims, "When about seven or eight I was a genuine pagan, so intoxicated with the beauty of Greece that I acquired a half-sincere belief in the old gods and Nature-spirits."

His mother apparently attempted another round of Sunday school when the boy was twelve, but this was as

> "WHEN ABOUT SEVEN OR EIGHT I WAS A GENUINE PAGAN,
> SO INTOXICATED WITH THE BEAUTY OF GREECE..."
>
> ~H. P. Lovecraft

unsuccessful as before. Lovecraft was "the despair of the institution," as he notes with pride:

> None of the answers of my pious preceptors would satisfy me, and my demands that they cease taking things for granted quite upset them.... At last I saw that they were hopelessly bound to unfounded dogmata and traditions, and thenceforward ceased to treat them seriously. Sunday-School became to me simply a place wherein to have a little harmless fun spoofing the pious mossbacks.

Not surprisingly, he was again allowed to drop out. In later years Lovecraft became a vigorous advocate for atheism, although chiefly only in letters and privately printed essays.

But another trauma was looming on the horizon. Whipple Phillips's health was failing, chiefly because of some business troubles. He had spent a substantial amount of money in constructing a dam over the Bruneau River, in Idaho. This dam collapsed twice, in 1890 and in early 1904. These events apparently caused a breakdown in Whipple's health, and he suffered a fatal heart attack on March 28, 1904. Worse was to come: shortly after his death, his estate was mismanaged by his executors, with the result that all that was left of the family fortune was the sum of $25,000, of which $5,000 went to Susie and $2,500 to Lovecraft. As a result, Lovecraft and Susie had to give up the grand family home and move to smaller quarters in a duplex at 598 Angell Street, a few blocks down the street.

The loss of his birthplace was, by his own testimony, the single most traumatic event of Lovecraft's young life. The illness and death of his father had occurred too early in his life to make much of an impression. But his rambling and cavernous birthplace, although not a historically or architecturally notable structure, had come to represent contentment and stability, and his moving into a "congested, servantless home" was almost too much for the boy to bear.

The final straw came when his beloved cat, Nigger-Man (a common name for black cats at the time), whom he had obtained as early as 1893, ran away in the course of their move from one house to the other, never to be seen again. The loss of this adored feline (the only pet Lovecraft ever owned) symbolized the loss of his birthplace as no other event could.

If we are to believe his later letters, Lovecraft actually contemplated suicide at this time. He would take long bicycle rides to the Barrington River, far to the east of his new house, pondering its weed-grown depths and wondering what it might be like to rest placidly at its bottom. What stopped him? He himself tells the story:

> And yet certain elements—notably scientific curiosity and a sense of world drama—held me back. Much in the universe baffled me, yet I knew I could pry the answers out of books if I lived and studied longer. Geology, for example. Just *how* did these ancient sediments and stratifications get crystallised and upheaved into granite peaks? ... What of the vast gulfs of space outside all familiar lands—desert reaches hinted of by Sir John Mandeville and Marco Polo ... Tartary, Thibet ... What of unknown Africa?

This is a defining moment in the life of H. P. Lovecraft. It was not family ties, religious beliefs, or even the urge to write that kept him from suicide, but scientific curiosity. In later years Lovecraft professed to an "acute, persistent, unquenchable craving TO KNOW," and he spent a lifetime in seeking to satisfy that craving. For the moment, his desires would have to be satisfied by the simple expedient of attending high school.

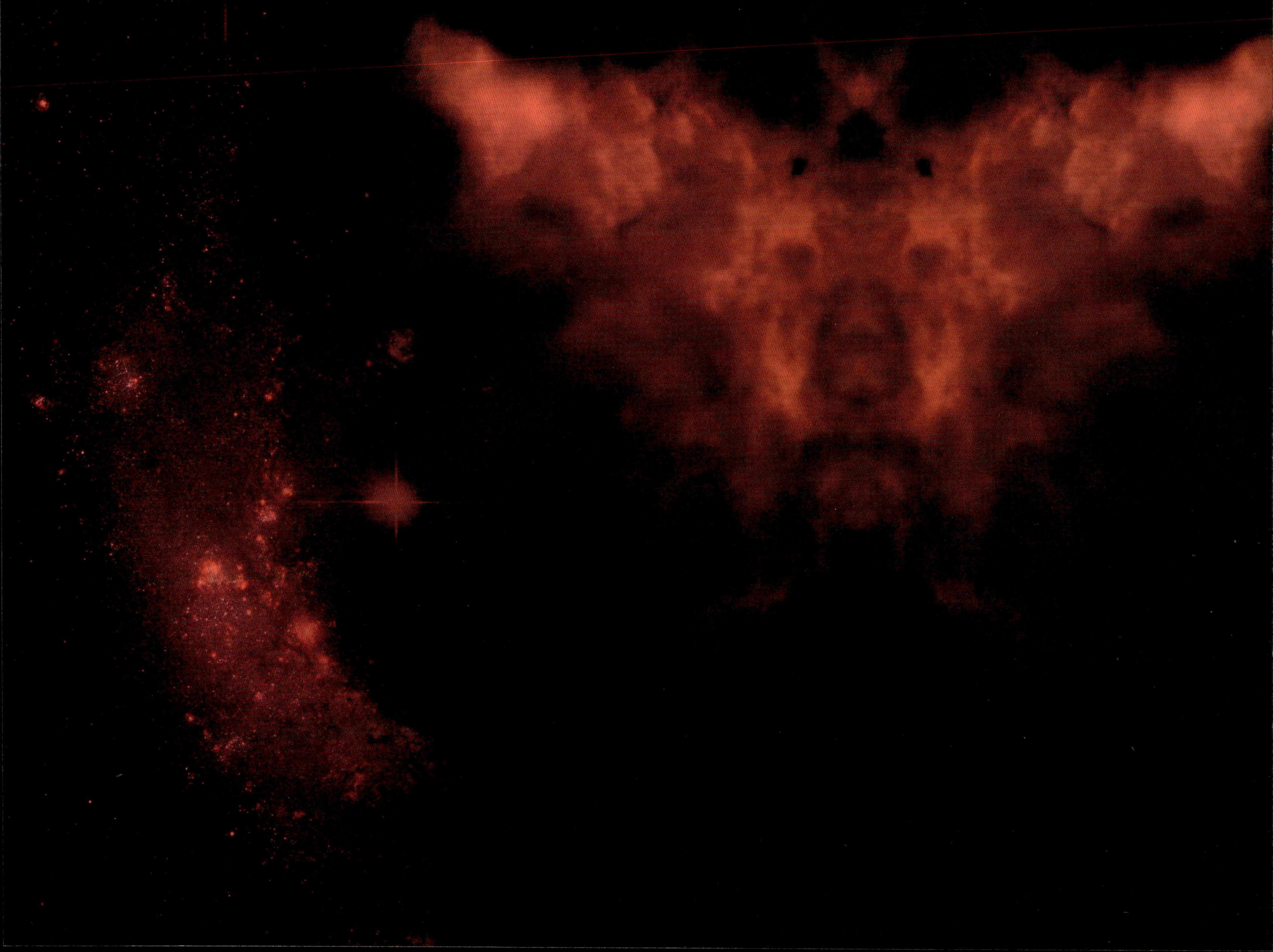

2

ECCENTRIC RECLUSE

(1904–1914)

To his and his family's surprise, Lovecraft ended up enjoying his high school years, despite his sporadic attendance. He attended the 1904–05 term with an unusual number of absences and returned in September 1905, but was withdrawn on November 7 and remained out for the rest of the term, not returning until September 1906. Evidently the rigors of attending school on a daily basis were still a bit too much for the nervous boy, and it was felt prudent to let him withdraw temporarily. He returned for the 1907–08 term, withdrawing permanently on June 10, 1908.

Lovecraft's high school transcript survives, and it is full of interest. He excelled in the sciences, getting an 85 in Botany and a 95 in both Physics and Chemistry. Some of his grades are surprisingly low; for example, he got only a 77 in English. Possibly he already knew much of the subject and found himself bored. More disturbing were his low grades in Elementary Algebra (74) and Intermediate Algebra (75), although he did well in Plane Geometry (92).

Lovecraft completed only three years of high school, if even that, and of course he did not receive a diploma, thereby wrecking his plans to attend nearby Brown University. This failure was deeply humiliating, and it resulted in one of the few instances where Lovecraft demonstrably lied to his friends and colleagues. In a later letter he wrote: ". . . after all, high-school was a mistake. I liked it, but the strain was too keen for my health, and I suffered a nervous collapse in 1908 immediately after graduating, which prevented altogether my attending college." For one who so valued the life of the mind, this lack of even a high school diploma was so shameful that he could not face it.

And yet, Lovecraft did a great many other things during the years 1904–08 aside from attending school. After the death of his grandfather and the move to 598 Angell Street, he made valiant efforts to pick up the threads of his life, both intellectually and emotionally. He and his friends resurrected both the Providence Detective Agency and the Blackstone Military Band. He also resumed his homemade scientific publications, including the *Scientific Gazette* and the *Rhode Island Journal of Astronomy*.

An intriguing ad in a 1905 issue of the latter paper describes Lovecraft and his friend Chester Munroe as leaders of the Blackstone Orchestra ("fine music cheap"). Another ad refers to a "New Repertoire–Tenor & Baritone Solos." Can it be that Lovecraft was attempting to sing? It certainly appears so. As he wrote in a 1918 letter: "Something over a decade ago I conceived the idea of displacing Sig. Caruso as the world's greatest lyric vocalist, and accordingly inflicted some weird and wondrous ululations upon a perfectly innocent Edison blank." (These blank wax cylinders were one of the earliest methods for recording music.) We would pay much to have these recordings today, but Lovecraft states, "I saw to it that an accident soon removed the incriminating evidence."

This period is also the heyday of the Great Meadow Country Clubhouse. This was a small wooden house with a stone chimney that Lovecraft and his friends found in the village of Rehoboth, Massachusetts, about eight miles east of Providence; it had been built by an old Civil War veteran, James Kay, and with his help the boys built an addition that was larger than the house itself. They brought tables, pictures, tar paper for the walls, and other accoutrements. The house and addition have now collapsed, but the chimney remains standing.

Lovecraft could be something of a smart aleck in high school. He was fond of telling the story of an English

RIGHT: *Lovecraft's transcript from Hope Street High School.*

ECCENTRIC RECLUSE

35

Astronomy
January: 1904

Combined with the Monthly Almanack
Price: 5¢

> "THE NAME 'PHILLIPS' IS A MAGIC WORD IN WESTERN RHODE ISLAND, AND THE *GLEANER* WAS MORE THAN WILLING TO PRINT AND FEATURE ANYTHING FROM WHIPPLE V. PHILLIPS'S GRANDSON."
>
> —H. P. Lovecraft

teacher, Mrs. Blake, who questioned the originality of a paper that the boy had turned in. Lovecraft brazenly admitted that it was copied verbatim from a newspaper article. As Mrs. Blake became increasingly indignant at the apparent plagiarism, Lovecraft pulled out the clipping: "Can the Moon Be Reached by Man? By H. P. Lovecraft."

In other words, Lovecraft had broken into print. His first published piece was a letter to the editor of the *Providence Journal*, published on June 3, 1906; it concerned a point of astronomy. A few months later he was thrilled to see another letter on astronomy published in the August 25, 1906, issue of the prestigious *Scientific American*.

Lovecraft also began two different astronomy columns for local papers, one for the *Pawtuxet Valley Gleaner* and one for the *Providence Tribune* (morning, evening, and Sunday editions).

The *Gleaner* articles began on July 27, 1906, and proceeded monthly until at least the end of the year. These articles cover a wide array of subjects pertaining to astronomy that Lovecraft believed to be of interest to general readers; the article on "Can the Moon Be Reached by Man"

LEFT: *The cover of* Astronomy Combined with the Monthly Almanack (*January 1904*), *another of Lovecraft's juvenile periodicals.*

ECCENTRIC RECLUSE

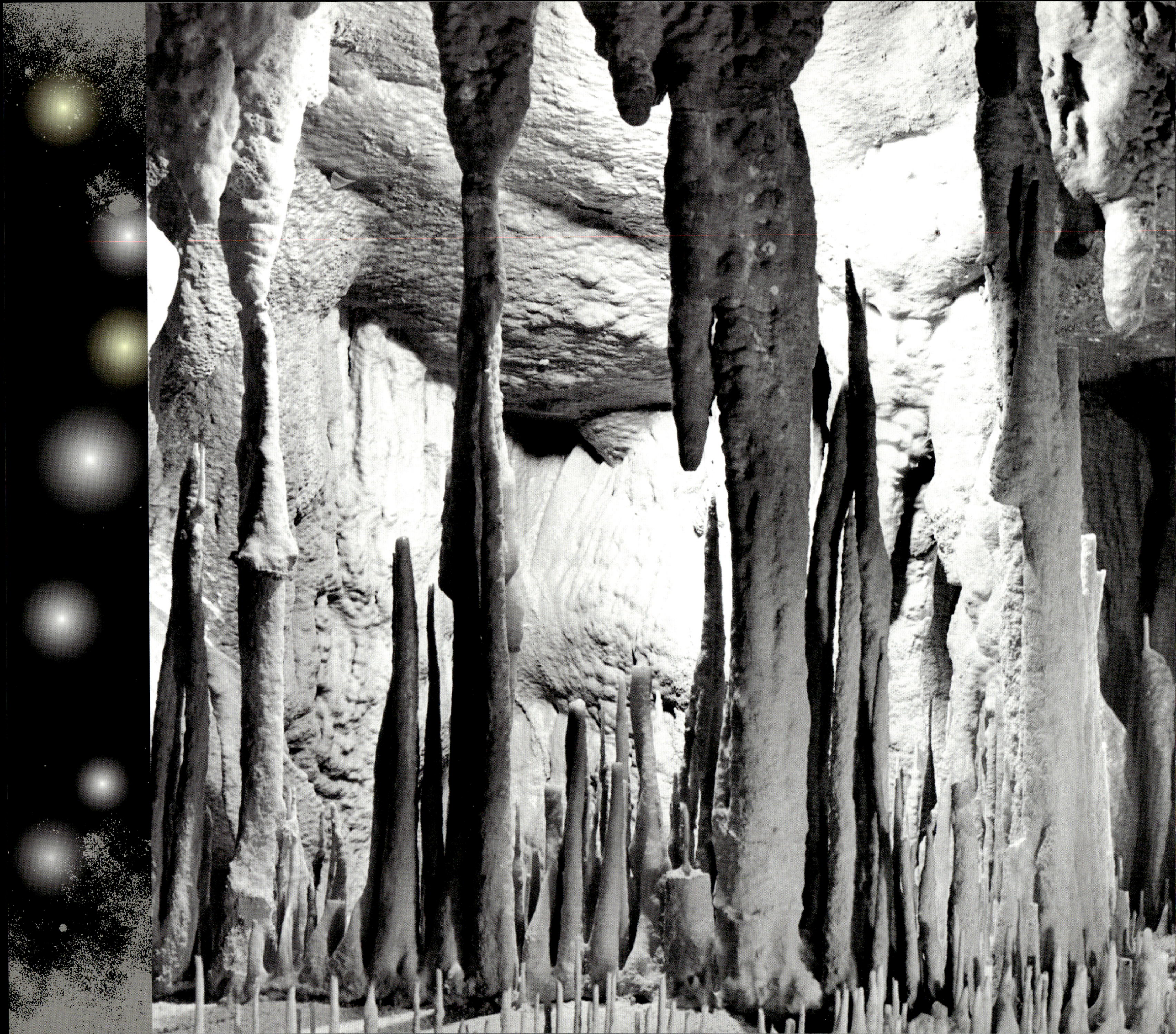

appeared in the issue of October 12, 1906. Other subjects include: "Is Mars an Inhabited World?"; "Is There Life on the Moon?"; and "Are There Undiscovered Planets?"

The *Gleaner* was published in a western suburb of Providence then known as Pawtuxet and now incorporated into the city of West Warwick. Lovecraft notes that "the name 'Phillips' is a magic word in Western Rhode Island, and the *Gleaner* was more than willing to print and feature anything from Whipple V. Phillips's grandson."

The articles for the *Providence Tribune* were published near the beginning of each month, and describe the more noteworthy astronomical phenomena for the month. They are not as interesting as the more speculative *Gleaner* articles, but they do feature Lovecraft's hand-drawn star charts—one of the few occasions when artwork by Lovecraft was published. These articles come to an abrupt end on June 1, 1908, the same time as his withdrawal from high school.

But of much greater interest for most readers today is the fact that, during this period, Lovecraft wrote large numbers of short stories and poems. Regrettably, only two survive, and they may not be representative of what he wrote during his high school years.

"The Beast in the Cave" was begun before Lovecraft and his mother had to vacate 454 Angell Street, but was not completed until April 21, 1905. It tells of a man lost in the depths of Mammoth Cave in Kentucky. He encounters a strange, shambling beast that, in the blackness of the cave, he does not see but only hears. In attempting to protect himself from the creature, he hurls rocks at it, fatally injuring it. The final sentence tells the whole story: "The creature I had killed, the strange beast of the unfathomed cave was, or had at one time been, a MAN!!!"

This conclusion is not likely to be much of a surprise to any reader, but the story as a whole is miles beyond "The Mysterious Ship" (1902). Although the story's prose is stiff, the gradual buildup of suspense and terror is effective, and the underlying theme of regression along the evolutionary scale is one that figures in many of Lovecraft's later stories.

The only other tale of this period that survives is "The Alchemist," written in 1908. This story is much more influenced by the old-time Gothic novel than "The Beast

LEFT: *Mammoth Cave in Kentucky, the inspiration for Lovecraft's story "The Beast in the Cave."*

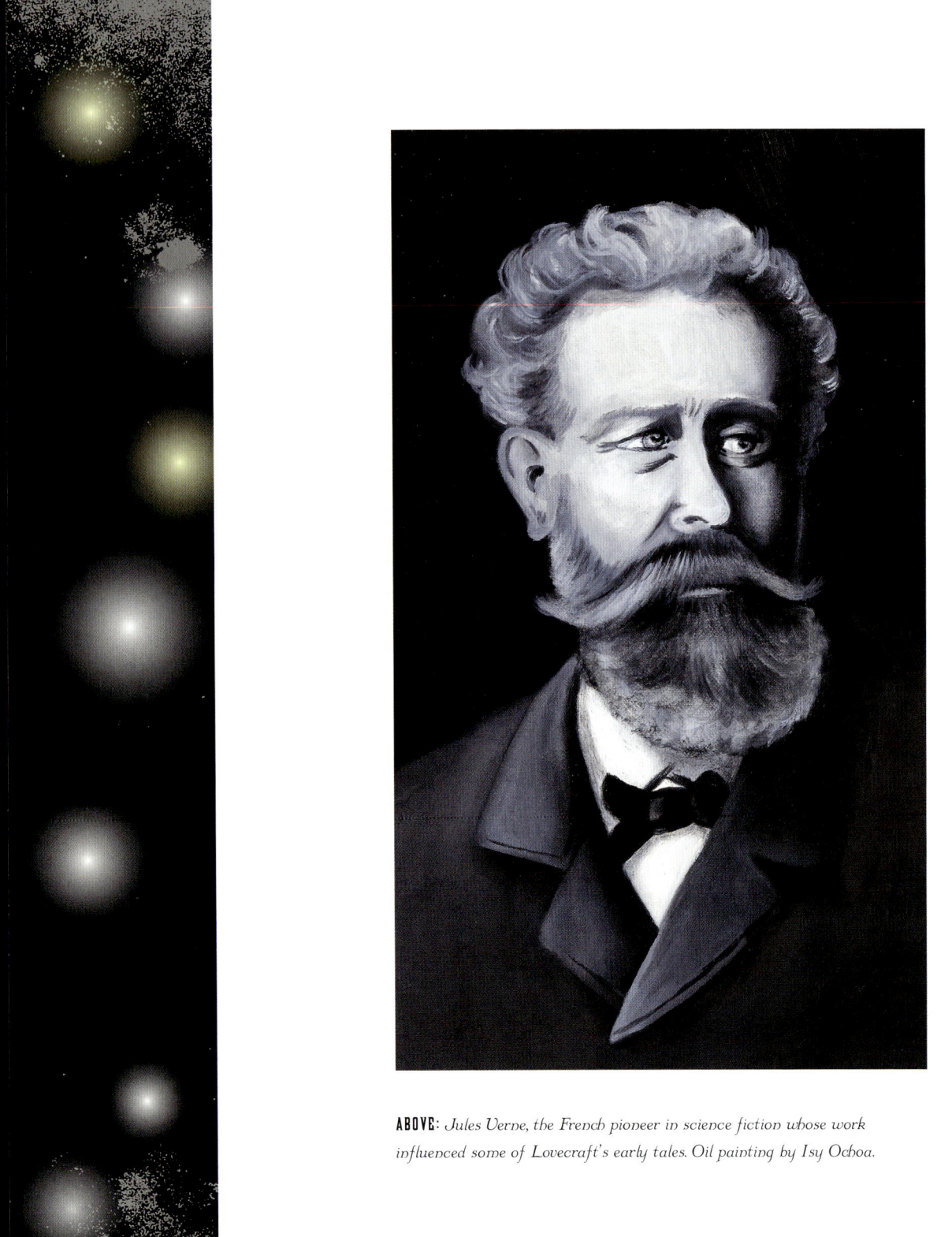

ABOVE: *Jules Verne, the French pioneer in science fiction whose work influenced some of Lovecraft's early tales. Oil painting by Isy Ochoa.*

in the Cave," presenting the narrative of the last of the Comtes de C—, an aristocrat living in a castle in France. Each one of his ancestors has died before the age of thirty-two, and in the end he finally learns the cause. In the thirteenth century an alchemist named Michel Mauvais was killed by Godfrey, the young son of the Comte de C—, and Michel's son, Charles le Sorcier, has extended his life unnaturally to exact vengeance upon all the subsequent counts.

Lovecraft clearly wrote many other stories during this time, but they do not survive. One intriguing specimen was called "The Picture" (1907); in a letter he states that this story was about "a man in a Paris garret [who painted] a mysterious canvas embodying the quintessential essence of all horror." Another was a kind of historical narrative about a Roman colony that was established in Central America. Lovecraft also seems to have written stories inspired by Jules Verne and detective tales modeled upon the Sherlock Holmes stories of Sir Arthur Conan Doyle. But in 1908 he destroyed all his stories of the previous five years except "The Beast in the Cave" and "The Alchemist." There is no indication that he ever made any efforts to submit even these stories for publication.

Of his poetry we have only a single example, and that

is an unfortunate one. "De Triumpho Naturae: The Triumph of Nature over Northern Ignorance" (1905) is a racist poem inspired by a contemporary treatise, William Benjamin Smith's *The Color Line: A Brief in Behalf of the Unborn* (1905). Smith makes the curious argument that the freeing of African slaves will doom them to extinction, because their innate "vice" will cause them to be afflicted with diseases, causing them to die out. If only they had remained as happy and contented slaves! Lovecraft's twenty-four-line poem is a versified condensation of Smith's argument ("Against God's will the Yankee freed the slave / And in the act consign'd him to the grave").

The issue of Lovecraft's racism—the one black mark on his character and his intellect—is one that we shall have to face throughout this book. It is clear that many of his views on African Americans, Jews, and other minorities were inculcated by his family, who, as members of old-time New England aristocracy, must have looked with alarm at the increasing prevalence of non-WASPs in their community and the nation as a whole. The period from 1890 to 1920 saw a massive influx of immigrants into the country, especially from southern and eastern Europe, Latin America, and Asia; the fact that these immigrants looked and behaved very differently from the English, German, and Scandinavian arrivals of an earlier period caused great concern among nativists who were worried about a nation that was changing before their eyes.

Throughout his life, Lovecraft tended to scapegoat "foreigners" for the broader social changes—increasing urbanization and industrialization; increasing commercial success on the part of immigrants who thereby challenged the social supremacy of WASPs—that were transforming the nation into a much more cosmopolitan place. And in terms of his prejudice against African Americans, Lovecraft believed he had science on his side on deeming them an "inferior" race: many reference works of the period made similar claims. It was only the pioneering anthropological work of Franz Boas and his disciples in the early decades of the twentieth century that destroyed forever the notion of the biological superiority or inferiority of the various human races of the world. Today, the very notion of "race" as a meaningful means of categorizing the human population is in question.

Lovecraft's abrupt withdrawal from high school initiated a five-year period of self-imposed isolation that was not lifted until late 1913. It is only during this time that he can legitimately be referred to as an "eccentric recluse," a term that some critics have used to refer to the entirety of Lovecraft's life. The shame of his lack of a high school diploma exhibited itself in a number of ways. He terminated his astronomy columns and gave up fiction writing. He also ceased going to Ladd Observatory, a small observatory owned by Brown University to which Lovecraft had been allowed access as early as 1903, when he first began developing an interest in astronomy. (In later years he professed that he had a perpetual crick in his neck from many hours of looking through Ladd's telescope.) Lovecraft paints a bleak picture of his life during this juncture:

> When I was 18 I suffered such a breakdown that I had to forego college. In those days I could hardly bear to see or speak to anyone, and liked to shut out the world by pulling down dark shades and using artificial light.

But what exactly *caused* this mental and psychological breakdown? Lovecraft provides us with only hints of an answer, but one very likely possibility is that his relatively poor marks in mathematics made a career as an astronomer impossible. For someone who had developed such a nearly professional interest in, and knowledge of, astronomy, this must have been a severe blow. Lovecraft comes close to admitting such a thing in a letter of 1931:

> In studies I was not bad—except for mathematics, which repelled and exhausted me. I passed in these subjects [in high school – but just about that. Or rather, it was *algebra* which formed the bugbear. Geometry was not so bad. But the whole thing disappointed me bitterly, for I was then intending to pursue *astronomy* as a career, and of course advanced astronomy is simply a mass of mathematics. That was the first major set-back I ever received—the first time I was ever brought up short against a consciousness of my own limitations. It was clear to me that I hadn't brains enough to be an astronomer—and that was a pill I couldn't swallow with equanimity.

We have only tantalizing glimpses of what Lovecraft was doing during this period. He rather pathetically revived the *Scientific Journal* and the *Rhode Island Journal of Astronomy* in early 1909. An "astronomical notebook" for the period 1909–15 survives and fills nearly one hundred pages, but it is very spotty: there are no observations at all for the years 1911 and 1913, although Lovecraft did write a lengthy description of Halley's Comet on May 26, 1910.

At some point during these years Lovecraft took a correspondence course in chemistry from the International Correspondence Schools of Scranton, Pennsylvania—a course that cost $161.00, a substantial sum for a young man and his mother who had no regular source of income. But although he was good in inorganic chemistry, the rigors of organic chemistry were too much for him: "I found myself so wretched bored that I positively could not study for more than fifteen minutes without acquiring an excruciating headache which prostrated me completely for the rest of the day."

This raises the issue of Lovecraft's employment. Once he realized that he could not be a professional astronomer or chemist, his family should have had him trained in some clerical or other white-collar occupation that could at least bring in some income to allow him to do his writing on the side. But this was never done. Lovecraft himself seems to have taken a cavalier attitude toward

RIGHT: *Illustration of a rocket capsule from the 1872 edition of Jules Verne's* From the Earth to the Moon.

ECCENTRIC RECLUSE

earning a living—a legacy, perhaps, from his childhood, when his family had no money worries—and he felt he "could always sell a story or poem or something" to bring in a few dollars. Even this, as he would later discover, proved to be difficult, especially for one who regarded writing merely as an elegant amusement.

We should also consider the domestic difficulties that Lovecraft faced. He lived alone with his mother at 598 Angell Street from 1904 to 1919, and it is clear that Susie Lovecraft was undergoing a slow decline in her psychological stability. She had been traumatized by the unsavory illness and death of her husband, however little she (or, for that matter, his doctors) may have known about the specifics of his condition. And the relatively small sum left to her and her son by Whipple Phillips created a sense of encroaching financial ruin that ultimately broke her down. It did not help that, in 1911, her brother, Edwin, lost a large sum of her money, apparently through bad investments.

One of the most painful incidents in Lovecraft's life may have occurred at this time, as recorded by Clara Hess, a neighbor who knew both Susie and her son. When Clara called on Susie at 598 Angell Street, "Mrs. Lovecraft talked continuously of her unfortunate son who was so hideous that he hid from everyone and did not like to walk upon the streets where people could gaze at him." It is shocking to think that any mother would say such a thing about her only son, but it was clearly a function of the strange love-hate relationship that had developed between the two. (Clara Hess pointedly notes that Susie "was considered then to be getting rather odd.")

The relations between Susie and Howard Lovecraft had been curious from the beginning. When the boy was two years old, Susie had told a friend that she should stoop when holding his arm, lest she pull it out from its socket. She seemed to indulge his every whim, giving him books, a chemistry set, and a telescope as he continued to explore new interests. But there is also evidence that she was emotionally remote from her son, rarely expressing her affection for him and withholding any physical demonstrations of intimacy. It may also be significant that, according to the later testimony of his wife, Lovecraft's sexual feelings were at their height when he was eighteen and nineteen years old—a development that Susie could not have welcomed.

RIGHT: *598 Angell Street, Providence, where Lovecraft resided from 1904 to 1924.*

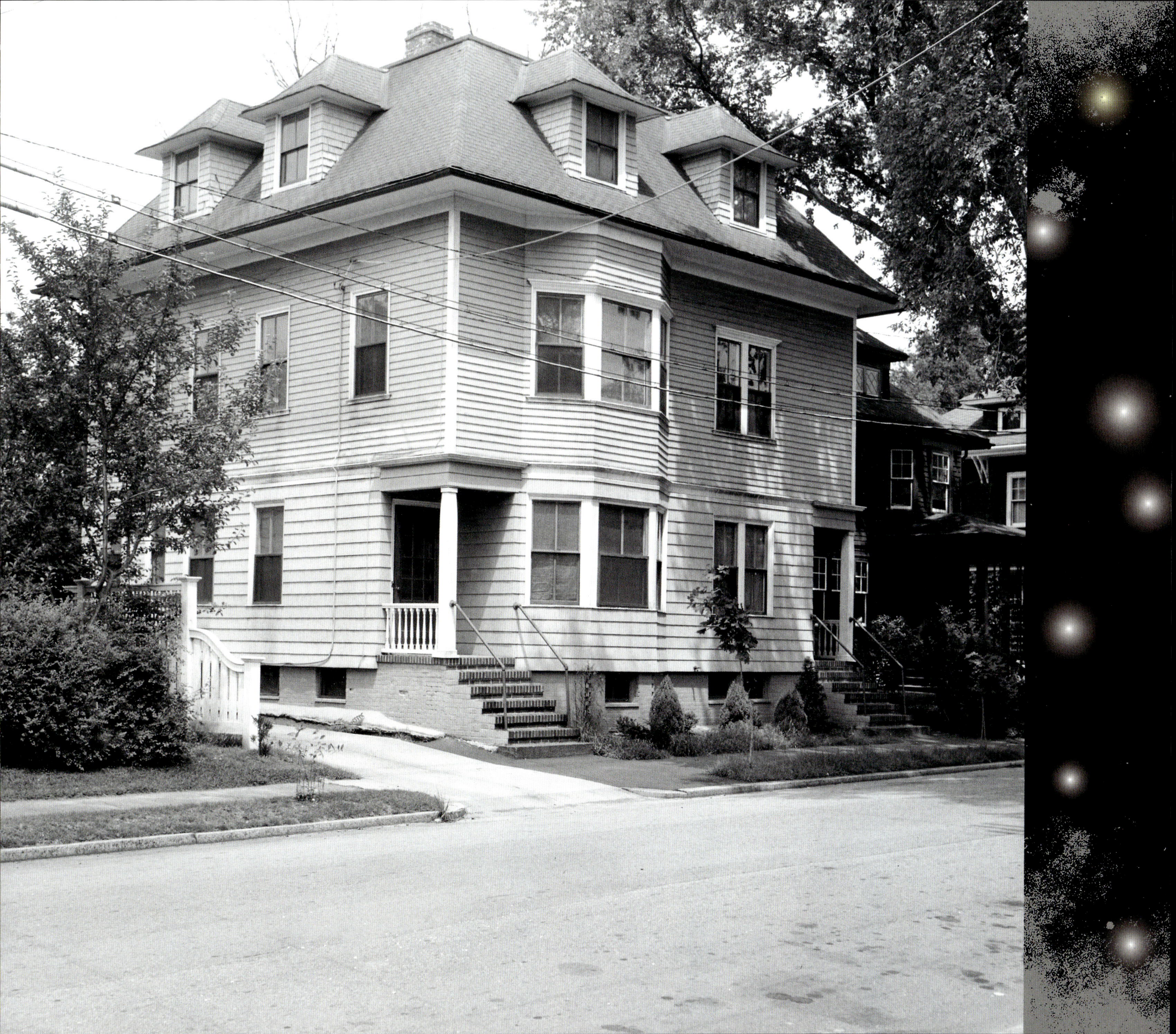

#37757

Know All Men:

I, Howard P. Lovecraft of the city of Providence in the State of Rhode Island, being of sound mind and memory, make, execute and declare this instrument as my last will, hereby revoking any and all former wills by me at any time heretofore made.

First: I direct that my executor pay out of my estate all my just debts and funeral expenses.

Second: All the rest, residue and remainder of my property and estate, real, personal and mixed, however described and wherever situated, of which I die seized and possessed, or in or to which at the time of my decease I have any right, title or interest, I give, devise and bequeath to my mother Sarah S. Lovecraft - To Have and To Hold the same unto and to the use of herself and her heirs and assigns forever.

Third: In case my said mother should not be living at the time of my decease, I give, devise and bequeath said rest, residue and remainder of my property and estate absolutely and in fee simple, two thirds thereof to my aunt Lillie D. Clark, wife of Franklin C. Clark, of said Providence, and the remaining one third thereof to my aunt Annie E. Gamwell, wife of Edward F. Gamwell of the city of Cambridge in the State of Massachusetts, or in case either of my said aunts shall decease prior to my death without leaving any descendant living at the time of my death to take by representation such deceased's share in my residuary property and estate, I give, devise and bequeath such share to the other of them, or if she also shall have deceased prior to the time of my death, to the descendants of such other equally but per stirpes and not per capita.

Fourth: I hereby nominate, constitute and appoint my said mother Sarah S. Lovecraft sole executor of this my will, and if for any reason she should not serve or continue to serve my said aunt Lillie D. Clark, and if for any reason neither my said mother nor my said aunt shall serve or continue to serve Albert A. Baker of said Providence as sole executor hereof, and I hereby request and direct any and all courts taking probate hereof not to require any of said persons to furnish any surety on any bond, or to file any inventory or to return any account of my estate as such executor.

In Witness Whereof I have hereunto set my hand and seal and declared this to be my last will, in the presence of three witnesses, at Providence, Rhode Island, this *Twelfth* day of August, A. D., 1912.

Howard P. Lovecraft

Perhaps she saw in her son the same traits that had led her husband to such a loathsome end.

The five or six long years of hermitism from 1908 to 1914 are sparsely illuminated with random events such as Lovecraft's riding the trolley cars all day on his twenty-first birthday (August 20, 1911), and his making his one and only will on August 12, 1912. Around 1911, he made a shift away from science and back to literature. One result of this shift is his first published poem, "Providence in 2000 AD," appearing in the *Providence Evening Bulletin* for March 4, 1912. This poem, too, is sadly racist—or at least xenophobic—but at the same time it is an amusing satire. Its inspiration was the effort by Italian Americans in Providence to have a major thoroughfare, Atwells Avenue, renamed Columbus Avenue. The attempt was unsuccessful, but it led Lovecraft to write a pungent satire in which his native town has become entirely overrun with foreigners.

Other poems of the period harp on the same things with less good humor, including a vile composition called "On the Creation of Niggers" (1912) that Lovecraft actually duplicated on the hectograph. "New-England Fallen" (1912) laments the "foreign boors" who have entered the region. A little less offensive is "On a New-England Village Seen by Moonlight" (dated September 7, 1913), which lays more emphasis on the decline of agricultural life and the dominance of machinery than on the incursion of foreigners.

Lovecraft's emergence from hermitism occurred in a very peculiar fashion. From as early as 1903, he had taken to reading popular magazines such as the *Argosy*, *All-Story Weekly*, and others of the chain established by Frank A. Munsey. Some historians believe that these are the first pulp magazines; whether they are or not, they are among the first all-fiction magazines directed to a popular audience, and Lovecraft—for all his devotion to the classics of Greece, Rome, and eighteenth-century England—indulged in them as a guilty pleasure. The *Argosy* and *All-Story Weekly* were not specialized in terms of subject matter, but they did contain their share of horror, fantasy, and proto-science fiction stories.

In a letter to the editor of the *All-Story Weekly*, published in the issue of March 7, 1914, Lovecraft speaks of having read every issue of that magazine since it

LEFT: *Lovecraft made his only will in 1912, when he was still quite young.*

The enormous broad tires of the chariots and the padded feet of the animals brought forth no sound from the moss-covered sea bottom; and so we moved in utter silence, like some huge phantasmagoria, except when the stillness was broken by the guttural growling of a goaded zitidar, or the squealing of fighting thoats.

We traversed a trackless waste of moss which, bending to the pressure of broad tire or padded foot, rose up again behind us, leaving no sign that we had passed.

~A PRINCESS OF MARS,
EDGAR RICE BURROUGHS

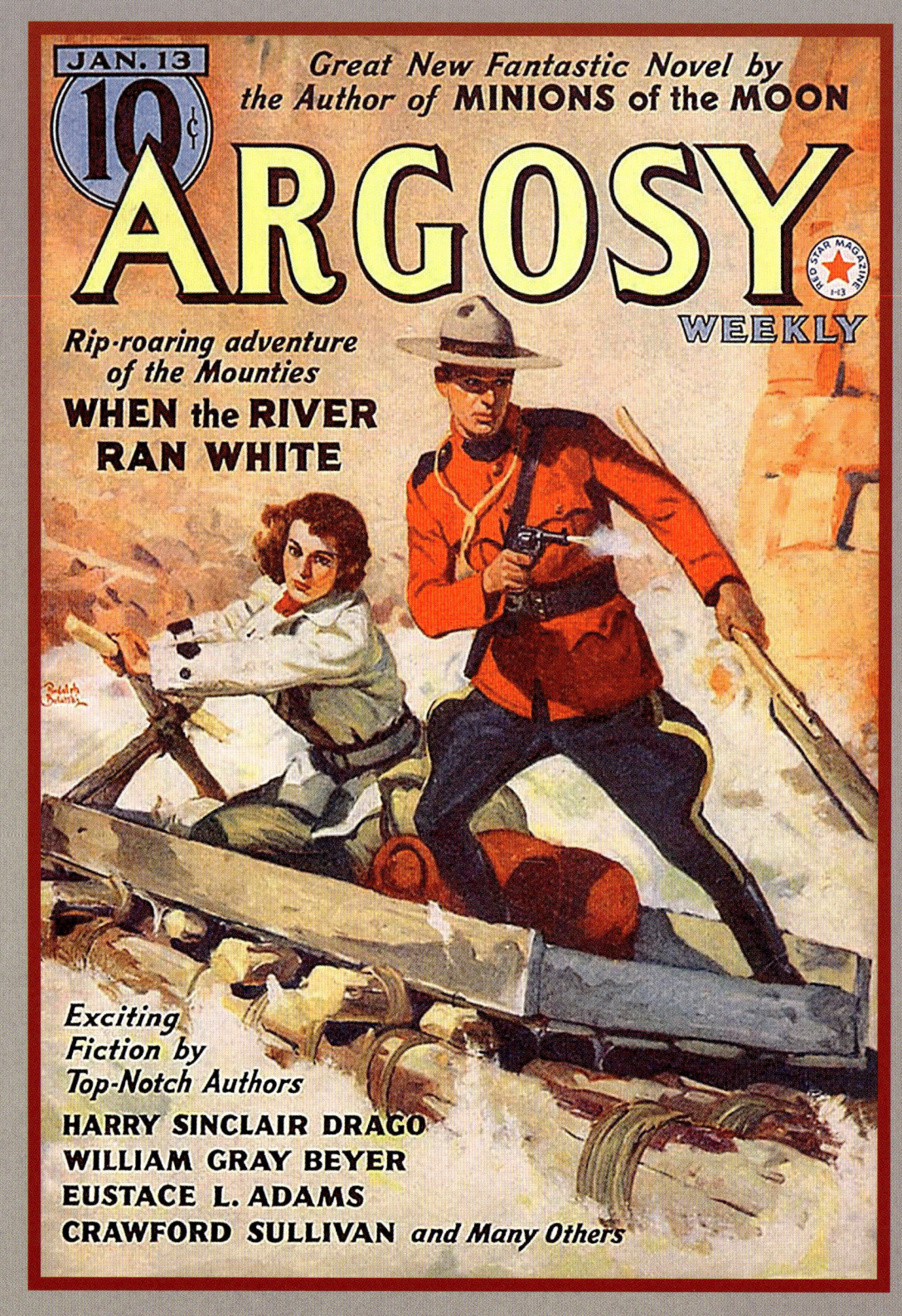

ABOVE: *The cover of the* Argosy Weekly *(January 13, 1940). Lovecraft read this magazine enthusiastically as a teenager for the Edgar Rice Burroughs adventure tales and the Westerns by Zane Gray.*

began in January 1905. He was particularly fond of the Tarzan and John Carter of Mars stories of Edgar Rice Burroughs, and he felt that in general the magazine "remains under the influence of the imaginative school of Poe and Verne." He also liked the historical tales of Albert Payson Terhune and the Westerns of Zane Grey.

But it was one writer of a very different sort in the *Argosy*, the romance writer Fred Jackson, who impelled Lovecraft to unleash his satirical pen. Jackson published numerous lengthy tales of romance and melodrama in issues of 1913 and 1914, and Lovecraft decided he had had enough. In a long letter published in the September 1913 issue, he condemned Jackson as a sentimentalist whose work did not belong in the magazine's pages.

Jackson was highly popular with readers, so a number of them wrote in to protest Lovecraft's censure of their favorite. One of these writers, John Russell of Tampa, Florida, wrote a pungent letter *in verse* poking fun at Lovecraft. This led Lovecraft to reply with a lengthy verse satire in the manner of Alexander Pope's *The Dunciad* (1728); he called it "Ad Criticos" ("To my critics"), and the first "book" appeared in the issue of January 1914. It begins engagingly:

What vig'rous protests now assail my eyes?
See Jackson's satellites in anger rise!
His ardent readers, steep'd in tales of love,
Sincere devotion to their leader prove;
In brave defence of sickly gallantry,
They damn the critic, and beleaguer me.

No doubt Lovecraft, lost as he was in antiquated modes of literary expression, did not consider it odd to resurrect a satirical style from two centuries before; but his screed only inspired Jackson's supporters to respond with greater outrage. The controversy went on for nearly a year, until the editor of the *Argosy* asked Lovecraft and Jackson to put an end to it by writing a joint poem that appeared in the October 1914 issue.

This whole contretemps was noticed by others outside the orbit of the magazine. In early 1914 Lovecraft received an invitation from Edward F. Daas to join the United Amateur Press Association. He did so on April 6, 1914, taking his first step out of self-imposed isolation. In a few years he would be transformed both as a writer and as a human being.

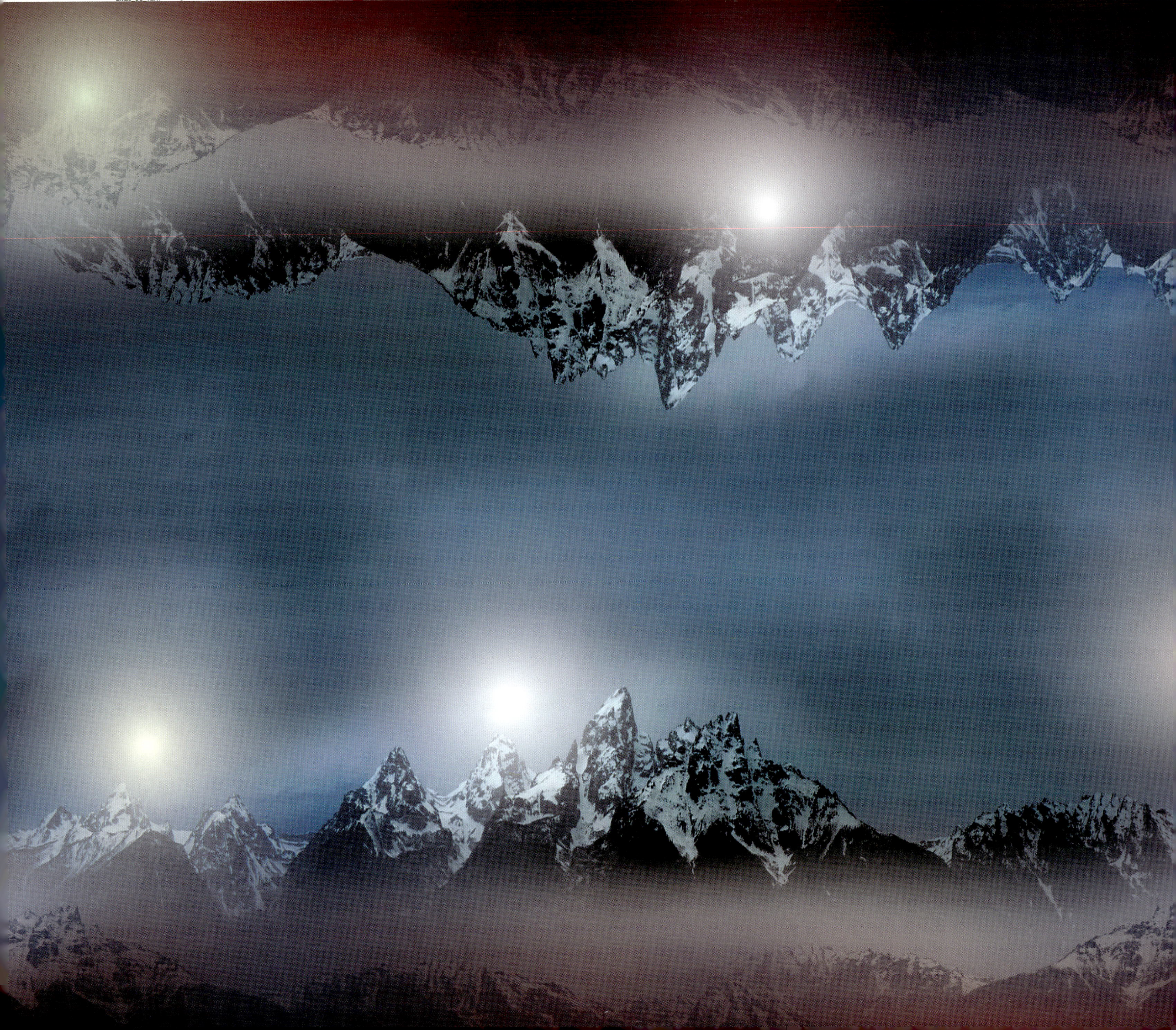

3

A RENEWED WILL TO LIVE

(1914–1924)

The world of amateur journalism that Lovecraft entered with such wide-eyed wonder in early 1914 was a curious institution, but very typical of its time in the emphasis on self-help, self-education, and the banding together of like-minded individuals. Organized amateur journalism began in 1876 with the founding of the National Amateur Press Association (NAPA); the publisher Charles Scribner and other notables in the fields of literature and publishing were initially involved, but over the years relatively few amateur journalists went on to become professional writers. This was largely because the hobby was focused not so much on writing as on printing. The magazines produced by amateurs fell somewhere between the literary "little magazines" of the day and the fanzines of a later period, but many amateurs enjoyed the process of setting type by hand and working with their own printing presses, oftentimes not caring much what they actually printed. It may have been for this reason that, in 1895, a fourteen-year-old boy named William H. Greenfield founded the United Amateur Press Association (UAPA) for the purpose of being more focused on the literary rather than the printing side of amateur journalism. Not every member produced his or her own magazine, of course; Lovecraft and many others enjoyed sending their contributions to a wide array of journals, thereby establishing relationships with members they knew only by correspondence.

Organized amateur journalism was rigidly hierarchical, with a president, vice president, secretary, and other officers elected for one-year terms. Elections were conducted at conventions held in July; those who could not attend the conventions in person could vote by proxy. Lovecraft frequently chided some members for being more interested in politics than in literature, especially given that the eminence of holding office was nothing to boast about: neither association ever had many more than 250 members scattered across the country, with a few more overseas.

As Lovecraft began sending out his initial contributions to amateur papers (his first, "A Task for Amateur Journalists," appeared in the *New Member*, July 1914), he strove to assess exactly what amateur journalism was and should be. In his mind, it was a forum for the exercise of literary skill

RIGHT: *A photograph of Lovecraft in 1915, published on the cover of the* United Amateur, *September 1915, during the period when he was vice president of the UAPA.*

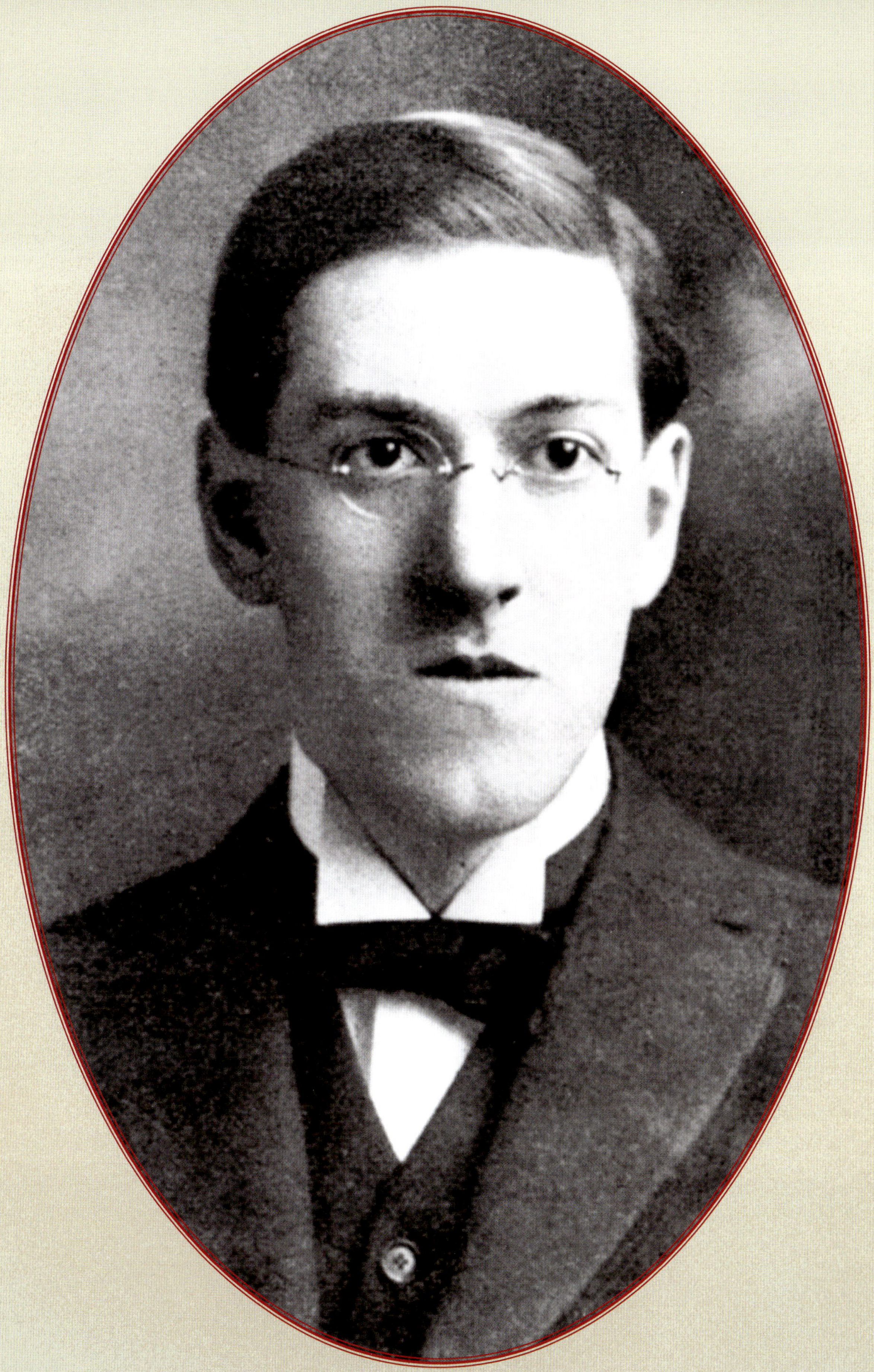

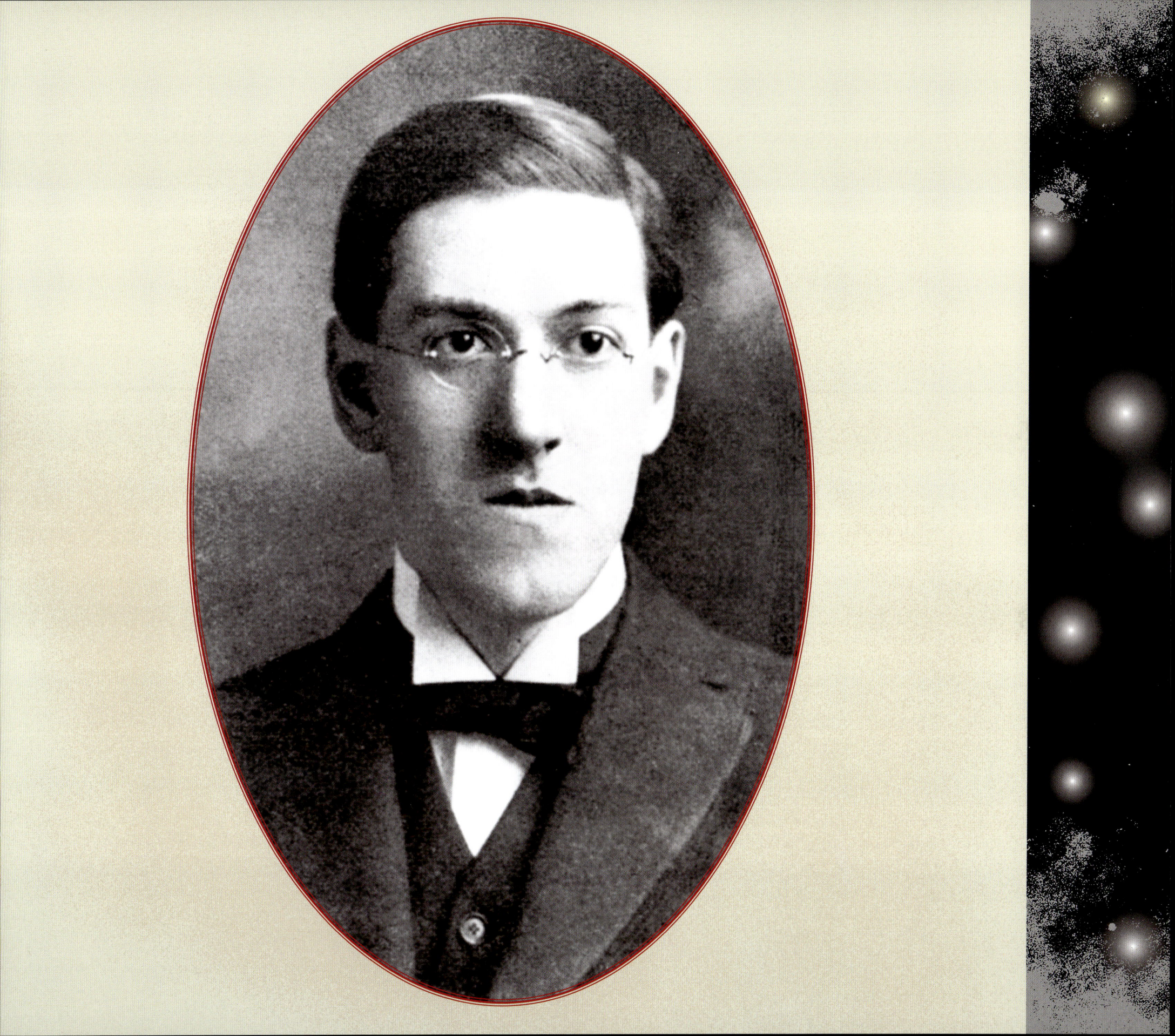

on a purely noncommercial basis. In this sense, it echoed his own chosen purpose for writing—abstract "self-expression" without thought of markets or payment. He based his own goals on the aristocratic eighteenth-century ideal of writing as an elegant amusement; as he wrote with tongue only half in cheek in a 1923 letter, "A gentleman shouldn't write all his images down for a plebeian rabble to stare at." It is doubtful that many amateurs of 1914 shared this belief.

Amateur journalism was exactly the right thing for Lovecraft at this critical juncture of his life. For the next ten years he devoted himself with unflagging energy to the amateur cause; for him it was not merely a hobby, but a full-time occupation. For someone so unworldly, so sequestered, and—because of his failure to graduate from high school—so diffident about his own abilities, the tiny world of amateur journalism was a place where he could shine. His knowledge and literary skills, self-taught as they were, were substantially greater than those of most other amateurs, and he quickly achieved distinction among their ranks. In the poignant essay "What Amateurdom and I Have Done for Each Other" (1921), he summed up the benefits he had derived:

Amateur Journalism has provided me with the very world in which I live. Of a nervous and reserved temperament, and cursed with an aspiration which far exceeds my endowments, I am a typical misfit in the larger world of endeavour, and singularly unable to derive enjoyment from ordinary miscellaneous activities. In 1914, when the kindly hand of amateurdom was first extended to me, I was as close to the state of vegetation as any animal well can be.... With the advent of the United I obtained a renewed will to live; a renewed sense of existence as other than a superfluous weight; and found a sphere in which I could feel that my efforts were not wholly futile.

Lovecraft gained an opportunity to help the amateur cause sooner than he expected: in late 1914 he was appointed chairman of the Department of Public Criticism. This office required Lovecraft to write a column in each issue of the "official organ," the *United Amateur,* subjecting the contributions of other members to critical scrutiny. Lovecraft was the chairman of this department for most

> "A GENTLEMAN SHOULDN'T WRITE ALL HIS IMAGES DOWN FOR A PLEBEIAN RABBLE TO STARE AT."
>
> –H. P. Lovecraft

of the next five years, and the columns, painfully mundane and at times hypercritical as they may appear, were probably what many amateurs needed. Lovecraft focused on obvious grammatical and stylistic problems in amateurs' writings, although occasionally he addressed issues of content as well. Most amateurs certainly did not follow his extremely conservative literary principles, which forbade the use of slang and colloquialism and looked only to "classical" models for prose and poetic composition. But Lovecraft stuck to his guns, writing several articles defending his views, such as "The Case for Classicism" (*United Co-operative*, June 1919) and "Literary Composition" (*United Amateur*, January 1920).

Lovecraft made an attempt to instruct amateur writers in a more hands-on way when he helped to form the Providence Amateur Press Club. This club comprised a small number of members who were attending night classes at a local high school. Most of the members were Irish, including a feisty young man, a year older than Lovecraft, named John T. Dunn. Lovecraft helped this group publish two issues of the *Providence Amateur* (June 1915 and February 1916), after which the group appears to have disbanded.

Much later, in 1975, L. Sprague de Camp interviewed Dunn about his relations with Lovecraft, and he provided some fascinating insights. De Camp writes: "Dunn found Lovecraft . . . odd or even eccentric. At gatherings Lovecraft sat stiffly staring forward, except when he turned his head towards someone who spoke to him. He spoke in a low monotone." Although they disagreed on many subjects, Dunn maintained that he liked Lovecraft. However, some other members of the club may not have been so friendly. One of the female members played a joke on Lovecraft by telephoning him and asking him out on a date. She probably knew that Lovecraft was very shy and withdrawn, and unaccustomed to dealing with women. Lovecraft soberly replied, "I'll have to ask my mother," but never returned her call.

Lovecraft's own contributions to amateur papers were, for several years, exclusively in the realm of essays, editorials, and poetry. Very little of this work is of intrinsic interest today, although it reveals much about the development of Lovecraft's mind and character. He began as a crabbed, bookish individual who expressed quick disdain for people and views he disagreed with, and his literary, political, and social conservatism is on full display. Indeed, he edited and published his own occasional journal, the *Conservative*, producing thirteen issues between 1915 and 1923, several of which were written entirely by himself. With the passing of time, he gained greater tolerance for opposing views, abandoned his exclusive devotion to classical literature, and learned the social skills to interact with friends and colleagues.

In the UAPA, Lovecraft took on various executive functions aside from his chairmanship of the Department of Public Criticism. He was elected first vice president for the 1915–16 term and president for the 1917–18 term. For much of the period from 1920 to 1925 he was the official editor of the UAPA, meaning that he edited the *United Amateur* and collected members' dues (usually $1 a year). As early as 1917, however, Lovecraft joined the NAPA, even though he had earlier exhibited hostility to its "boy printer" ideal. He confessed at the time that he did so because many other members believed that "my aloofness from the National was a barrier to inter-associational harmony." This remark testifies to the significant position Lovecraft occupied in the amateur world. He created

RIGHT: *Propaganda poster for US enlistment in World War I.*

something of a furor when he was appointed the interim president of the NAPA in 1922–23, after the elected president abruptly resigned.

It was of course impossible for anyone, even someone so cloistered as Lovecraft, to ignore events in the outside world, but when World War I broke out in the summer of 1914, Lovecraft made a surprising personal effort to join in the war effort. In May 1917, a few days before the United States finally did enter the war, he attempted to enlist in the Rhode Island National Guard. The physical examination he received was so cursory that he passed it, and he seemed duly enrolled in the Guard. His comments at this time are revealing:

> Some time ago, impressed by my entire
> uselessness in the world, I resolved to
> attempt enlistment despite my almost invalid

condition. I argued that if I chose a regiment soon to depart for France, my sheer nervous force, which is not inconsiderable, might sustain me until a bullet or piece of shrapnel could more conclusively and effectively dispose of me.

Quite frankly, there is some hyperbole here. Even if Lovecraft had remained in the Guard., he probably would not have been sent overseas; instead, he would likely have been stationed at Fort Standish in Boston Harbor. Nevertheless, his enlistment caused an uproar at home. He had clearly acted without his mother's knowledge or permission, and when she found out, she was, as he declares, "almost prostrated with the news, since she knew that only by rare chance could a weakling like myself survive the rigorous routine of camp life." Accordingly, Susie immediately pulled some strings and had Lovecraft declared unfit to serve on medical grounds. This whole incident speaks volumes for the breakdown in the relations between Lovecraft and his mother. For his part, Lovecraft admitted to feeling "desolate and lonely indeed as a civilian." He was of course obligated to register in the draft, doing so on June 5; but he was again declared unfit to serve in the Army, and so all he could do was write.

Lovecraft did write some poems on the war and other timely topics. Most of his dozens of poems written in the period 1914–21 were, however, on more abstract subjects, and nearly all of them were in an antiquated eighteenth-century idiom that he had adopted from his early readings of John Dryden, Alexander Pope, and other poets of the period. Lovecraft was, as he declared in 1929, well aware that the vast bulk of this poetic work was aesthetically inferior.

> In my metrical novitiate I was, alas, a chronic and inveterate mimic; allowing my antiquarian tendencies to get the better of my abstract poetic feeling. As a result, the whole purpose of my writing soon became distorted–till at length I wrote only as a means of re-creating around me the atmosphere of my 18th-century favourites.

To this there is very little to add. Lovecraft's poetry covers a wide range of subjects, including seasonal verse, poems addressed to other amateurs, and poems of a philosophical cast. The best of his verse may be his satirical poems, where Lovecraft exhibits a genuine zest for lampooning the literary, political, and other flaws of his friends—and of himself. "On the Death of a Rhyming Critic" (*Toledo Amateur*, July 1917) is a wonderful send-up of his own antiquated mannerisms, which by then had become a byword in the amateur world. Conversely, "Amissa Minerva" (*Toledo Amateur*, May 1919) is a pungent satire on what Lovecraft perceived to be the freakish eccentricity of contemporary poetry, with several poets such as Amy Lowell, Edgar Lee Masters, and Carl Sandburg cited by name.

Surprisingly, Lovecraft also resumed the writing of astronomy columns. He actually did so before entering amateur journalism, as a monthly column for the *Providence Evening News* began on January 1, 1914. Fifty-three monthly columns appeared until the column ended on May 2, 1918. This series is his most expansive astronomical work, and Lovecraft frequently explains the origin of mythological terms for the stars, planets, and constellations. A more basic series of articles, "Mysteries of the Heavens Revealed by Astronomy," appeared in the *Asheville Gazette-News* in 1915, apparently facilitated by Lovecraft's boyhood friend Chester P. Munroe, who now lived in Asheville, North Carolina.

Amidst all this work as a poet, essayist, and critic, would Lovecraft ever resume the writing of horror fiction? In 1915 he wrote to an amateur colleague, "I wish that I could write fiction, but it seems almost an impossibility." But matters slowly changed. He allowed his old story "The Alchemist" to appear in the November 1916 issue of the *United Amateur*. This story was read by W. Paul Cook, an amateur living in Athol, Massachusetts. Cook, who owned an extensive library of weird fiction, strongly urged Lovecraft to resume fiction writing, and Lovecraft complied in the summer of 1917, producing "The Tomb" and "Dagon" in short order.

These two stories are a study in contrasts. "The Tomb" could have been passed off as a lost story by Edgar Allan Poe. It tells of a young man, Jervas Dudley, who is psychically possessed by the spirit of an ancestor, Jervas Hyde, to such a degree that he exhibits knowledge of events in the remote past that he could not possibly know. The story's prose style is archaic and a bit stiff, testifying to Lovecraft's lack of practice.

"Dagon," on the other hand, is contemporary in its setting and general thrust. A sailor is captured by a German sea raider but escapes on a boat; he is stunned to discover, upon waking up one morning at sea, that a land mass has arisen all around him. Exploring this new terrain, he comes upon an obelisk with bizarre hieroglyphic carvings and then, to his horror, sees an immense and hideous creature, something like an enormous whale, that flings its scaly arms around the monolith in an act of worship. He later connects this sight to accounts of the Philistine fish-god Dagon. "Dagon" has an advanced, almost science-fictional atmosphere. Lovecraft suggests that the whalelike entity is only one of an entire race of creatures that dwells in the depths of the ocean, rendering humanity's rule over of the earth fragile and tentative indeed.

It took some time for Lovecraft to limber up his fictional pen: he wrote no more weird tales in 1917 and only one fantasy story in 1918. In 1919 he wrote six tales; in 1920, ten (the most prolific year of his career); in 1921, seven. These stories are a mixed bag and many of them are of little intrinsic interest, but they indicate how Lovecraft was experimenting in various fictional styles to see what worked best for him.

A good many of the stories of this period were inspired by his ecstatic discovery of Lord Dunsany, whose tales he first read in September 1919. He had known of Dunsany's work before, but felt that it was merely light fantasy of a sort that he did not care for; but when an amateur colleague lent him *A Dreamer's Tales* (1910), the first paragraph, as he stated years later, "arrested me as with an electric shock, and I had not read two pages before I became a Dunsany devotee for life."

As luck would have it, Lovecraft quickly got the chance to express his newfound admiration in person. Dunsany was conducting an extensive lecture tour across the United States in 1919–20, and on October 20, 1919, he gave a reading at the Copley Plaza in Boston. Lovecraft sat in the front row, taking pride in helping Dunsany put on his coat afterward. Lovecraft went on to read all of Dunsany's books, including his plays, short stories, and prose poems.

Lovecraft wrote close to a dozen tales in 1919–21 employing the prose-poetic language, the exotic settings, and the faux-naïf morality characteristic of Dunsany's work. Several, however, are far more than mere pastiches. Such stories as "The White Ship" (1919), a pensive allegory about the possibly futile quest for happiness, and "Celephaïs" (1920), a poignant tale of a man who, failing to find success in the real world, creates a world of his own imagination where he can reign as king, show Lovecraft using dreamlike fantasy to underscore a philosophical message. "The Terrible Old Man" (1920) is not customarily thought of as a Dunsanian story, but it was probably inspired by a tale in *The Book of Wonder* (1912). It is notable for being set in Kingsport, the first of Lovecraft's invented New England cities.

Lovecraft, of course, did not abandon supernatural horror in 1919–21. One of the most interesting tales is "The Statement of Randolph Carter" (1919), chiefly because of its genesis. It was the product of a highly detailed dream in which Lovecraft and Samuel Loveman, an amateur colleague whom he had not yet met in person, explore an ancient cemetery in New England. They dig up a grave, which reveals steps leading down into the depths of the earth; Loveman goes down, ordering Lovecraft to remain on the surface. They stay in touch by walkie-talkie, and in the end it is not Loveman's voice but another one that tells Lovecraft: "YOU FOOL, LOVEMAN IS DEAD!" Lovecraft narrated this dream in a letter; the story is an almost verbatim copy of the letter.

Another notable tale is "Facts Concerning the Late Arthur Jermyn and His Family" (1920). In a partial

ABOVE: *Lord Dunsany, the Anglo-Irish fantasist who influenced Lovecraft significantly in the years 1919–21.*

A RENEWED WILL TO LIVE

reprise of "The Beast in the Cave," we here encounter a British aristocrat who is horrified to discover that an ancestor had married a white ape from Africa and begotten a hybrid race of descendants exhibiting peculiar physiological and mental traits. This story may well have a racist subtext—a warning against "miscegenation," or racial interbreeding—but it remains a powerful tale. "From Beyond" (1920) is a crudely written but conceptually interesting story in which a mad scientist invents a machine that will "break down the barriers" erected by the five senses that limit our perception of phenomena. As a result, the scientist and his friend see hideous creatures all around them, drifting through their own presumably solid bodies.

The most interesting tale of 1920, however, is "The Picture in the House." Here Lovecraft not only invents the imaginary city of Arkham, which would play so large a role in his later fiction, but portrays both his love and terror of old New England. A bicyclist encounters a loathsome backwoods denizen living in a remote house outside of Arkham. It turns out that this man has lengthened his life far beyond the norm (he was actually born in the eighteenth century) by cannibalism. The rich texture of this story, and its authentic evocation of the history and topography of New England, make it one of Lovecraft's early triumphs.

"The Music of Erich Zann" (1921) remained one of Lovecraft's favorites, chiefly for its smooth-flowing prose and for the tantalizing indefiniteness of its supernatural scenario. Erich Zann, a mute German musician, seems to be playing his viol (the Renaissance instrument held between the knees like a cello) in a maniacal effort to prevent some force or entity from entering through the window of his garret apartment; but the narrator, who pulls back the curtain, sees only "the blackness of space illimitable." There is an artistic restraint in this story that contrasts starkly with the flamboyance of many of Lovecraft's other early tales.

Of "The Outsider" (1921) it is difficult to speak in small compass. This tale has been rightly regarded as one of Lovecraft's signature compositions, and many have seen it as deeply autobiographical. Here we are told of a creature who has lived, apparently alone, in a castle

RIGHT: *Lovecraft's hand-drawn map of his imaginary town of Arkham, Massachusetts. The town provided the setting for many of Lovecraft's stories and has taken on a life of its own in pop culture.*

A RENEWED WILL TO LIVE

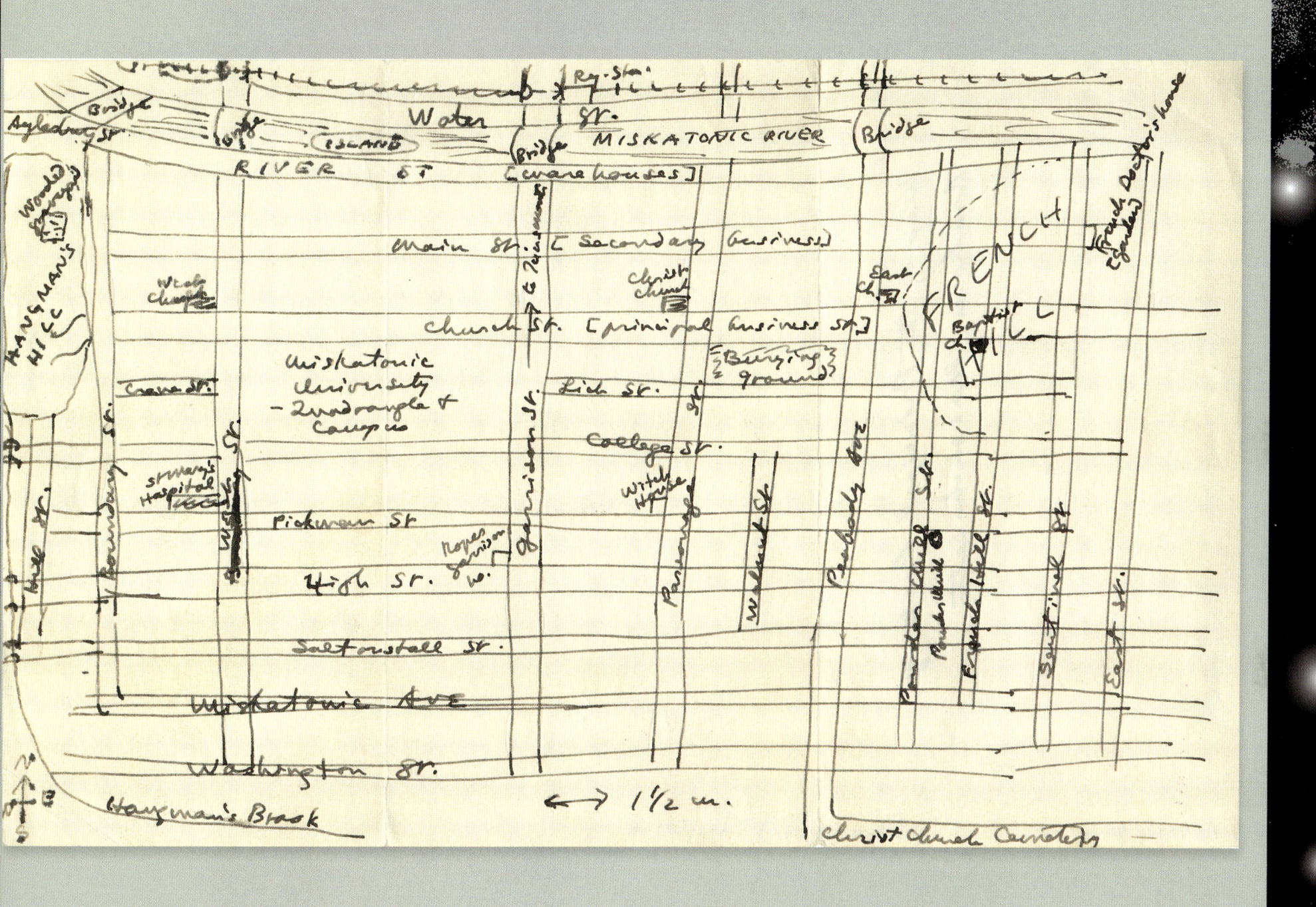

> "I KNOW ALWAYS THAT I AM AN OUTSIDER; A STRANGER IN THIS CENTURY AND AMONG THOSE WHO ARE STILL MEN."
>
> ~"The Outsider"

without mirrors. He yearns to see the light and climbs the tallest tower of the castle, only to discover that he has reached the solid ground. Walking along a path, he sees another castle in the distance, where a party is taking place. Entering through a window, he is stunned to find the partygoers fleeing madly. Out of the corner of his eye he sees a hideous entity. Unable to prevent himself from approaching it, he is shattered by the knowledge that the creature is none other than himself: in reaching out to the monster he ends up touching a mirror.

This tale is so heavily Poe-inspired (chiefly by such stories as "Berenice" and "The Masque of the Red Death") that it becomes debatable how autobiographical it really is. Does it reflect Lovecraft's own low self-esteem about his appearance, given that his mother once referred to him as "hideous"? This interpretation seems a bit facile, and the tale has broader significance than that: it is a poignant exhibition of the mind-destroying effects of knowledge. But its final words~"I know always that I am an outsider; a stranger in this century and among those who are still men"~may well be a true reflection of Lovecraft's own sense of alienation from modern society at this period in his life.

It is interesting to note that Lovecraft actually resumed weird writing in poetry before he did so in prose.

"The Poe-et's Nightmare" (1916) is a three-hundred-line poem that, although outwardly humorous, contains a section that enunciates the central theme of Lovecraft's creative work—cosmicism, or the insignificance of all human life amidst the temporal and spatial infinity of the universe. "Psychopompos: A Tale in Rhyme" (1917–18) is an engaging but relatively conventional narrative poem about werewolves. A number of other weird poems were written in the period 1917–20 and probably constitute the most significant and interesting facet of Lovecraft's poetic output.

One of the greatest benefits Lovecraft derived from amateur journalism was that he encountered friends and colleagues with whom he could engage both intellectually and emotionally. It was through the influence of these friends that he also began venturing out into the world, finally ridding himself of the hermitism in which he had been mired since his withdrawal from high school. Even more significantly, his intellectual horizons were widened by contact with people who thought and felt very differently from the way he did.

At the start, these friends were friends only by correspondence, but Lovecraft nonetheless established strong

ABOVE: *Rheinhart Kleiner, one of Lovecraft's closest friends in amateur journalism.*

and lifelong bonds with them. Among them were such individuals as Rheinhart Kleiner, a poet of light verse who lived in Brooklyn; Maurice W. Moe, a schoolteacher in Wisconsin; W. Paul Cook, who has already been discussed as instrumental in encouraging Lovecraft to resume fiction writing; Samuel Loveman, a refined poet in Cleveland whose greatest work, *The Hermaphrodite* (1926), is an exquisite evocation of classical Greece; and Alfred Galpin, a brilliant young man in Wisconsin who was first a pupil of Moe's but developed into a bold and original thinker who discussed philosophy, politics, and other issues with Lovecraft.

Lovecraft was still hesitant to venture out into the world (he once said that he never spent a single night away from home between 1901 and 1920), so some of these friends came to visit him. Both Kleiner and Cook paid a call on Lovecraft in the summer of 1917, and their accounts of his family life are fascinating. Cook tells of meeting Lovecraft's mother, who "was very cordial and even vivacious, and in another moment had ushered me into Lovecraft's room." He goes on to say: "Every few minutes Howard's mother or his aunt, or both, peeped into the room to see if he had fainted or shown signs of strain." Kleiner adds an interesting note: "I noticed that at every hour or so his mother appeared in the doorway with a glass of milk, and Lovecraft forthwith drank it." This coddling was something Lovecraft had probably endured so long that he failed to notice it.

But trouble was in the offing. Lovecraft's uncle by marriage, Franklin Chase Clark, who had married his aunt Lillian in 1902, died in 1915, and his paternal uncle, Edwin E. Phillips, died in 1918. Aunt Annie had separated from Edward F. Gamwell around 1916. This left Susie with no male member of the family to rely on, and in early 1919 her health broke down. She seems to have suffered a major nervous breakdown that eventually required hospitalization. She entered Rhode Island Hospital in March 1919 and never emerged. Her death on May 24, 1921, was caused by a gall bladder operation from which she could not recover.

This whole period was a severe strain on Lovecraft; whatever his actual feelings about his mother, he seems to have regarded her as a symbol of stability and continuity. The death of Susie Lovecraft momentarily inspired thoughts of suicide on Lovecraft's part ("For two years she had wished for little else [than death]—just as I myself wish for oblivion"), but he snapped out of these lugubrious thoughts quickly. He couldn't know then that her absence from his life would ultimately liberate him to become the man and the writer he wished to be.

For one thing, Lovecraft was able to travel a bit more widely. In 1920 he made several trips to the Boston area to visit with amateur writers. One of them, Winifred Virginia Jackson, although fourteen years his elder, joined Lovecraft in so many activities (coediting amateur papers, getting together at amateur conventions, and so forth) that rumors developed of a budding romance. It seems very unlikely that Lovecraft himself had much of a romantic interest in Jackson, although he did write her a few flattering poems. The two writers also collaborated on two weird stories, "The Green Meadow" and "The Crawling Chaos," but these stories amount to little.

In July 1921 he visited Boston again, this time for the NAPA convention, where he met Sonia H. Greene for the first time. Sonia, a Russian Jewish immigrant, had been married at least once before, but by this time she was either divorced or a widow, living in Brooklyn. She was a successful executive in a New York department store, specializing in hat making. Although she was seven years older than

ABOVE: *Sonia Haft Greene, who became Mrs. H. P. Lovecraft in 1924.*

Lovecraft, a mutual attraction immediately sprang up. Sonia, in the fascinating memoir she wrote after Lovecraft's death, noted bluntly, "I admired his personality but frankly, at first, not his person"–a clear reference to Lovecraft's very plain looks.

Sonia took the initiative, visiting Lovecraft in Providence in September. Incredibly, she managed to persuade him to visit her in Brooklyn, on the excuse that he could then meet Samuel Loveman (who was in town looking for work) and numerous other friends he had in the area. It was an offer too good to refuse, so on April 6, 1922, Lovecraft boarded a train and reached the metropolis a few hours later.

New York was a revelation to Lovecraft. In his first view of Manhattan, it seemed like a fairy kingdom rising magically out of the water. Aside from meeting friends, his six-day trip was full of sightseeing, bookstore hunting, and all the other things that most tourists of a bookish sort do when they hit the big city. Sonia, who had turned her Brooklyn apartment over to Lovecraft and Samuel Loveman while she stayed with a neighbor, seemed keen on pursuing a relationship. On one occasion, Lovecraft paid a great deal of attention to the neighbor's cat. Sonia commented, "What a lot of perfectly good affection to waste on a mere cat, when some woman might highly appreciate it!" Lovecraft replied, "How can any woman love a face like mine?" To which Sonia responded, "A mother can, and some who are not mothers would not have to try very hard." This remark was somewhat unfortunate, given Susie Lovecraft's cruel jab about Lovecraft's "hideous" face, but it suggests that Sonia wanted to take the relationship to a deeper level.

She moved things along by encouraging Lovecraft to spend several days with her in the Massachusetts resort towns of Gloucester and Magnola in late June and early July. This was the first time that Lovecraft ever spent any significant time alone with a woman who was not a relative. One night Sonia, seeing the full moon over the water, came up with an idea for a horror story. Lovecraft encouraged her to write it, and with his help she wrote a mediocre sea-monster story called "The Horror at Martin's Beach," later published in *Weird Tales* as "The Invisible Monster."

Lovecraft did not only travel to visit his women friends. Samuel Loveman lived in Cleveland, near Lovecraft's young friend Alfred Galpin; Lovecraft took a long train ride to Cleveland in late July and early August. It was the farthest west that he had ever been. He stayed for two weeks, then returned to New York for several more weeks in the city. It was at this time that he and Rheinhart Kleiner ventured to the cemetery of the Dutch Reformed Church in Brooklyn, where Lovecraft actually broke off a piece of an old Dutch tombstone. Thinking about his vandalism, he soon wrote the lurid story "The Hound," about an ancient ghoul who exacts revenge on two men who desecrate his grave. The story is so over-the-top that it may as well be a parody, with more chuckles than terrors.

Other friends and colleagues were appearing on the scene. One of the most important was Frank Belknap Long, with whom Lovecraft had begun corresponding in 1920. At that time Long was a young man of nineteen,

LEFT: *The New York skyline bordering the Hudson River circa 1921.*

We here behold a practically meaningless collection of phrases, learned allusions, quotations, slang, and scraps in general; offered to the public (whether or not as a hoax) as something justified by our modern mind with its recent comprehension of its own chaotic triviality and disorganisation.

—"RUDIS INDIGESTAQUE MOLES,"
H. P. LOVECRAFT

ABOVE: *T. S. Eliot, whose avant-garde poem* The Waste Land *did not suit Lovecraft's conservative tastes.*

eager to become a writer of weird fiction. He would eventually become Lovecraft's best friend. A more prominent figure who made Lovecraft's acquaintance at this time was the poet Hart Crane, later famous for writing *The Bridge* (1930), an avant-garde poem about the Brooklyn Bridge. Crane was a friend of Samuel Loveman's and would meet Lovecraft several more times in the coming years.

Lovecraft at this time also sent a fan letter to the California poet Clark Ashton Smith. Smith had created a furor when, at the age of nineteen, he published a scintillating book of cosmic and fantastic poetry, *The Star-Treader and Other Poems* (1912). Under the tutelage of another California poet, George Sterling, Smith published several more volumes over the next decade. He never attained a national reputation, but he was lionized in his native state. Lovecraft found his poetry transcendently brilliant and wrote Smith to tell him so. Smith would later become a noted writer of fantasy and horror tales.

Contact with people like Long and Smith seems to have inspired Lovecraft to revise some of his antiquated views of art and literature. Some of his later amateur articles reveal a surprisingly tolerant view of contemporary literature. In response to an amateur who was advocating censorship, he noted that such works as James Branch Cabell's *Jurgen* (1919) and James Joyce's *Ulysses* (1922)—the first of which came close to being banned in the United States, the second of which was actually banned—were "significant contributions to contemporary art."

But there were limits to his tolerance. When T. S. Eliot's modernist poem *The Waste Land* (1922) was published, Lovecraft condemned it in no uncertain terms, writing in the essay "Rudis Indigestaque Moles" (*Conservative*, March 1923) that it was "a practically meaningless collection of phrases, learned allusions, quotations, slang, and scraps in general; offered to the public (whether or not as a hoax) as something justified by our modern mind with its recent comprehension of its own chaotic triviality and disorganisation." Lovecraft went on to write a hilarious parody of Eliot's poem, entitled "Waste Paper: A Poem of Profound Insignificance." It was almost the only free-verse poem he ever wrote.

Lovecraft was finally venturing, tentatively, into the world of professional publication. He had had some poems published professionally as early as 1917, in such magazines as the *National Magazine* (Boston) and the *National Enquirer* (a temperance paper). But he seemed

ABOVE: *Clark Ashton Smith, one of Lovecraft's closest colleagues, began as a poet. Thanks to Lovecraft's influence, he branched out into fantasy horror fiction, becoming a major contributor to* Weird Tales.

content to publish his short stories in the amateur press. That changed when an amateur colleague, George Julian Houtain, came up with the idea of starting a humor magazine, *Home Brew*, that would also contain some horror fiction. He asked Lovecraft to write a series of "Grewsome [sic] Tales," telling his friend: "You can't make them too morbid." Lovecraft complied with a six-part serial, "Herbert West–Reanimator," published in *Home Brew* from February to July 1922.

To be frank, "Herbert West–Reanimator" is close to the nadir of Lovecraft's fiction, although it could be redeemed by thinking of it as something of a parody. Its premise–Dr. Herbert West seeks a chemical formula that can revive the recently dead, with loathsome results–is elementary, and each segment becomes progressively more lurid and preposterous. It is not surprising that this flamboyant and over-the-top tale served as the basis for the campy 1985 horror film *Re-Animator*. For this work Lovecraft was paid the princely sum of $5 a segment, or $30 in all. Late in 1922 he wrote another serial in four parts, "The Lurking Fear." This is somewhat better–it is another tale of hereditary degeneration, as a family in upstate New York resorts to interbreeding and becomes a

> "I PAY NO ATTENTION TO THE DEMANDS OF COMMERCIAL WRITING."
>
> –H. P. Lovecraft

race of molelike creatures—but still nothing to brag about. This *Home Brew* serial (January–April 1923) is enlivened by line drawings by Clark Ashton Smith, one of Lovecraft's closest colleagues for the last fifteen years of his life.

Lovecraft's ability to earn money was otherwise pretty feeble. As early as 1917 he had started the only remunerative occupation he ever held: he called it "revision," and by this he meant everything from light copyediting to wholesale ghostwriting. Although some of the horror tales that Lovecraft revised or ghostwrote have become famous, the revision of fiction was a relatively small portion of his work; instead, he was tasked with revising poetry, textbooks, articles, and other miscellaneous literary work.

In many ways, however, this was the worst kind of work for someone like Lovecraft to take up. Firstly, the rates he charged were very low; as late as 1933, he was asking only $2.50 a page for full ghostwriting (based on a synopsis provided by the would-be author), when he should probably have been asking double or triple that amount, given the amount of time and effort he spent on the task. Secondly, this revision work was too much like original fiction, so that he was left with little time or energy for the writing of his own tales. Since he also spent many hours a day writing

ABOVE: *Cover of* Weird Tales, *the magazine that published the great majority of Lovecraft's tales.*

letters to his ever-growing cadre of correspondents, it is no surprise that Lovecraft usually wrote only one or two stories a year in the last decade of his life.

One of the most reliable, if annoying, of Lovecraft's revision clients was the Reverend David Van Bush, who in the early 1920s became a successful author of pop psychology and self-help books. He called on Lovecraft to bring some kind of coherence both to his nonfiction books as well as to the truly awful poetry he attempted to write. Lovecraft hated the work, but it brought in a reliable income, so he was forced to stick with it. He met Bush in Cambridge, Massachusetts, in June 1922, when Bush was lecturing there. He wrote pungently: "[Bush] is actually an immensely good sort–kindly, affable, winning, and smiling. Probably he has to be in order to induce people to let him live after they have read his verse."

The opportunity for a regular professional market for his fiction emerged with the founding of *Weird Tales*. This legendary pulp magazine, which published a remarkable 279 issues over the next thirty-one years, was the brainchild of J. C. Henneberger, a publisher who had already achieved success with the magazine *College Humor*. The first issue of *Weird Tales* appeared in March 1923, edited by Edwin Baird; several of Lovecraft's friends urged him to submit to it. He reluctantly did so that summer, sending in five stories and including a cover letter that pointedly noted that "I pay no attention to the demands of commercial writing" and adding that the issues of the magazine he had seen "are more or less commercial—or should I say conventional?—in technique, but they all have an enjoyable angle." Baird impishly published this letter in the September 1923 issue. He said he would consider Lovecraft's tales if he resubmitted them in double-spaced typescripts; Lovecraft, who hated typing with a passion, grudgingly complied. Baird accepted all five stories, and the first one, "Dagon," appeared in October 1923.

Lovecraft's tortured relationship with *Weird Tales* is difficult to describe in a small space. There is no question that the vast majority of fiction published in the magazine was formula work that has little lasting literary merit; but mainstream markets were becoming increasingly closed to weird literature, since this type of writing was regarded as inferior to the social realism—typified by the work of F. Scott Fitzgerald and Sinclair Lewis—that dominated the literary world at the time. Authors like Lovecraft, Clark Ashton Smith, and Robert E. Howard had little choice but to submit to *Weird Tales*. It paid, on the whole, about a penny a word; Lovecraft claimed that he received a higher rate, about a penny and a half. He quickly became one of the early stars of the magazine, and he also took pride in convincing Edwin Baird to open up the magazine to weird poetry.

Lovecraft at this juncture also discovered the weird writing of Welsh author Arthur Machen, whose work was enjoying popularity in the United States thanks to reissues of his books by Alfred A. Knopf. Lovecraft was particularly taken with the story collection *The House of Souls* (1906), the episodic novel *The Three Impostors* (1895), and the sensitive autobiographical novel *The Hill of Dreams* (1907). Machen's influence stands behind only Poe's and Dunsany's in Lovecraft's work, and it becomes evident in such a story as "The Festival," written in late 1923.

This story is based on a trip that Lovecraft had taken in December 1922 to the town of Marblehead, Massachusetts, along the North Shore just north of Salem. Lovecraft had been to Salem several times, but he was told that Marblehead was a town of even finer colonial antiquities, so he made a trek there. Marblehead remains an exquisite haven of colonial architecture, and Lovecraft was enraptured. In 1930 he described his sentiments in a letter:

I looked, and a pang of horror seized my heart as with a white-hot iron. There upon the floor was a dark and putrid mass, seething with corruption and hideous rottenness, neither liquid nor solid, but melting and changing before our eyes, and bubbling with unctuous oily bubbles like boiling pitch. And out of the midst of it shone two burning points like eyes, and I saw a writhing and stirring as of limbs, and something moved and lifted up what might have been an arm.

~"NOVEL OF THE WHITE POWDER,"
ARTHUR MACHEN

ABOVE: *Arthur Machen, Welsh writer whose mystical tales of horror were relished by Lovecraft.*

In a flash all the past of New England–all the past of Old England–all the past of Anglo-Saxondom and the Western World–swept over me and identified me with the stupendous totality of all things in such a way as it never did before and never will again. That was the high tide of my life.

It took some time for Lovecraft to digest his impressions of Marblehead, but he finally did so in "The Festival." It is here that he identifies his imaginary town of Kingsport (invented in "The Terrible Old Man") with Marblehead, just as he would later identify Arkham with Salem. To this day one can trace the narrator's course through this archaic town. When, in conjunction with the townspeople, he descends through a trapdoor in a church to some underground realm, he encounters hideous winged creatures similar to the "Little People" of Machen's tales.

Just before writing "The Festival," Lovecraft wrote "The Rats in the Walls." This is without question the finest story of his first decade of writing. An American named Delapore refurbishes an ancestral estate in England, Exham Priory, but he and his pet cat are troubled by the sound of rats scurrying through the walls of the house. Eventually he and a band of scholars descend to the depths of the house, finding loathsome evidence that Delapore's family had committed unspeakable acts over the centuries, including cannibalism. Delapore instantly descends the evolutionary scale (a point cleverly suggested by the increasing archaism of his speech) and is found crouched over the half-eaten body of a friend. The power and richness of "The Rats in the Walls"–Lovecraft's version of "The Fall of the House of Usher"–cannot be overstated. It is his greatest tale of hereditary degeneration, but in this case the devolution happens instantly rather than over the course of generations. The tale is exquisitely modulated, beginning quietly but accumulating unnerving details and building relentlessly to a powerful climax.

But Lovecraft was doing more than writing the occasional weird tale. His correspondence with Sonia H. Greene had continued steadily for nearly three years, although they had visited each other only rarely. On March 2, 1924, he boarded a train from Providence to New York, and the next day, he married Sonia in a private ceremony at St. Paul's Chapel.

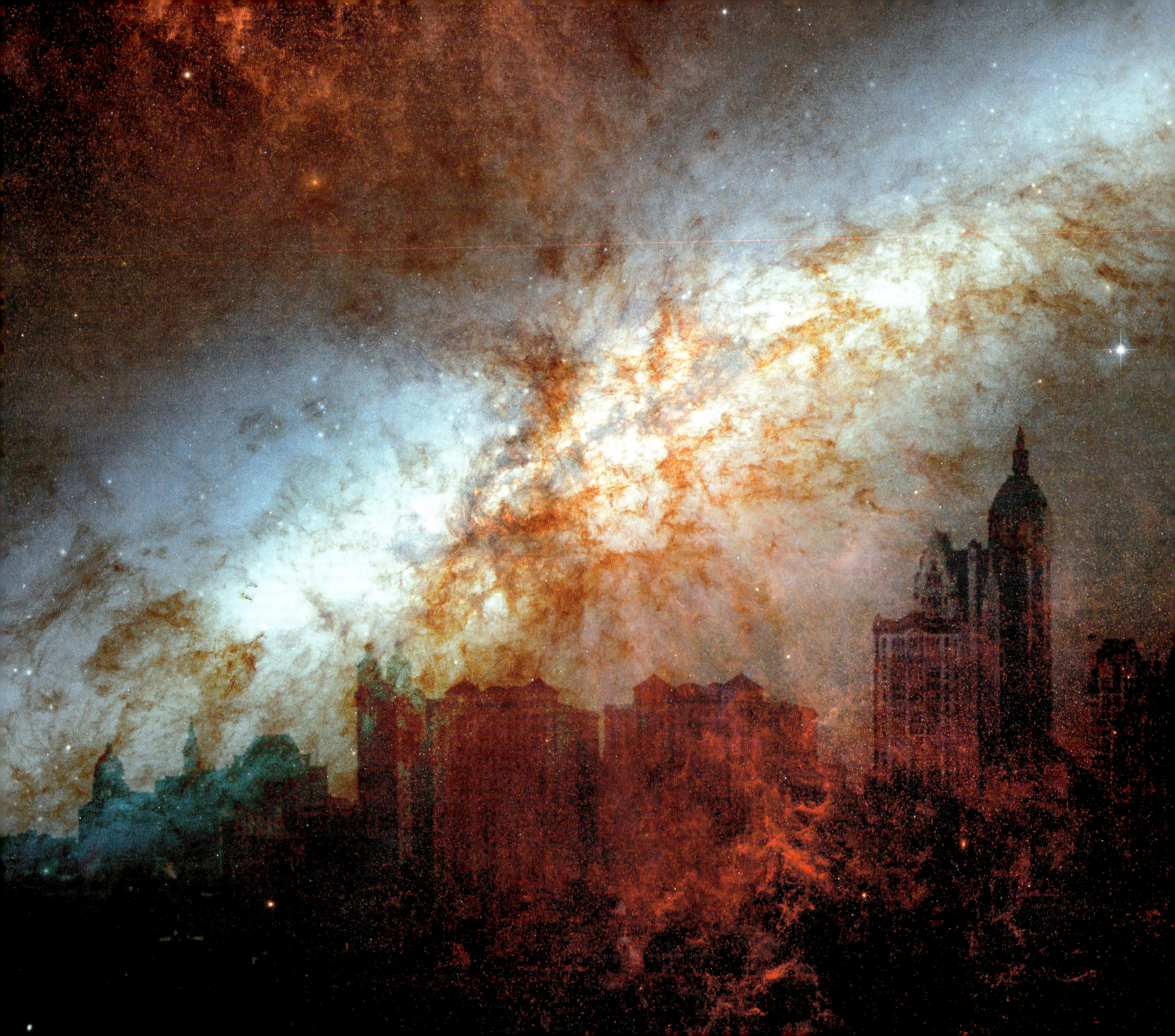

4

NEW YORK EXILE

(1924–1926)

One of the many remarkable things about Lovecraft's decision to marry Sonia is that he failed to tell his aunts, Lillian and Annie, about the matter until six days after the fact. It was only on March 9 that he wrote a long letter to Lillian outlining his reasons for this seemingly precipitate act. Here he states that a "more active life, to one of my temperament, demands many things which I could dispense with when drifting sleepily and inertly along, shunning a world which exhausted and disgusted me, and having no goal but a phial of cyanide when my money should give out." Well, perhaps marriage and a move to the big city are better than suicide from poverty and boredom!

What about the critical issue of the pair's affection for each other? Lovecraft goes on to say:

> Meanwhile—egotistical as it sounds to relate it—it began to be apparent that I was not alone in finding psychological solitude more or less of a handicap. A detailed intellectual and aesthetic acquaintance since 1921, and a three-months visit in 1922 wherein congeniality was tested and found perfect in an infinity of ways, furnished abundant proof not only that S. H. G. is the most inspiriting and encouraging influence which could possibly be brought to bear on me, but that she herself had begun to find me more congenial than anyone else, and had come to depend to a great extent on my correspondence and conversation for mental contentment and artistic and philosophical enjoyment.

This is one of the most glaring examples of Lovecraft's inability to speak of "love" or anything remotely like it—a point Sonia herself emphasized in her memoir when she noted that the closest Lovecraft could ever come was to say, "My dear, you don't know how much I appreciate you."

And yet, reading between the lines of this letter makes it evident that Lovecraft had a well-founded fear that his aunts did not approve of Sonia and of his marriage to her. It was for this reason that the couple essentially eloped. Sonia notes that she asked Lovecraft to inform his aunts before he left for New York, but he "preferred to surprise them."

What Lovecraft and Sonia had done was to conduct a long-distance romance—then, as now, a difficult endeavor.

RIGHT: *The marriage certificate for Lovecraft and Sonia Haft Greene. Lovecraft married her without telling his family.*

STATE OF NEW YORK.
CERTIFICATE AND RECORD OF MARRIAGE
of
Howard Phillips Lovecraft and **Sonia Haft-Greene**

No. of Certificate: 6276

	Groom		Bride
Residence	598 Angell St. Providence R.I.	Residence	259 Parkside Av. Brooklyn
Age	33	Age	40
Color	White	Color	White
Single, Widowed or Divorced	Single	Single, Widowed or Divorced	Widowed
Occupation	Writer	Maiden Name, if a Widow	Sonia Haft
Birthplace	Providence R.I.	Birthplace	Cherrigov, Russia
Father's Name	Winfield S.	Father's Name	Simon Haft
Mother's Maiden Name	Sarah S. Phillips	Mother's Maiden Name	Rachel Haft
Number of Groom's Marriage	1st	Number of Bride's Marriage	2nd

I hereby certify that the above-named groom and bride were joined in Marriage by me, in accordance with the Laws of the State of New York, at 29 Vesey (Street/Church), in the Borough of Manhattan, City of New York, this 3rd of March 1924.

Witnesses to the Marriage: Joseph Gorman, Joseph G. Armstrong

Signature of person performing the Ceremony: George B. Cox
Official Station: Curate
Residence: 29 Vesey

NEW YORK EXILE

It was wishful thinking that Lovecraft could speak of his three-month stay with Sonia in 1922 as testimony of their "perfect" compatibility, but it was perhaps understandable in one who was inexperienced in human relationships in general and intimate relationships with women in particular. That Sonia herself also seemed to harbor the same feelings, after having gone through at least one unsuccessful marriage, is more surprising.

Many have wondered how Lovecraft, who throughout his life exhibited bouts of anti-Semitism, could come to marry a Russian Jewish immigrant. But Lovecraft found certain members of minority groups objectionable only when they clung tenaciously to their own culture. Like many of his time, Lovecraft believed that immigrants were obligated to assimilate to the norms and standards of the dominant culture, and he felt that Sonia—who by all odds was a secular, cosmopolitan Jew thoroughly integrated into American life—was such a person. He felt the same about his Jewish friend Samuel Loveman.

Some have claimed that Lovecraft was simply looking for a mother replacement, pointing out that he first met Sonia six weeks after Susie Lovecraft's death. But this encounter was merely happenstance. Sonia was nothing like Susie Lovecraft. Susie was old-fashioned, emotionally reserved, and parochial, whereas Sonia was contemporary, emotionally open, and cosmopolitan. Although seven years older than Lovecraft, she was attractive and dynamic; it is clear that she pursued Lovecraft far more than Lovecraft pursued her. Some of his friends, such as Frank Belknap Long, believed that Sonia had asked Lovecraft to marry her, and he felt it would be ungentlemanly to turn her down.

Lovecraft's move to New York made a certain amount of sense, aside from any feelings for Sonia. If he seriously wished to become a professional writer, a move to the nation's center of publishing was logical. Moreover, Sonia was well established in a department store, Ferle Heller, where she made an income of $10,000 a year. This was a significant sum at the time, given that the average annual income of a family of four was about $2,000. So the couple would have had no money worries at the outset, and there was no immediate need for Lovecraft to seek employment. With luck, he could take his time establishing himself as a professional writer, slowly developing relations with editors and publishers.

RIGHT: *The early twentieth-century New York skyline as seen from the Manhattan Bridge.*

The marriage got off to an unusual start because of a rush assignment that J. C. Henneberger, owner of *Weird Tales*, had thrust upon Lovecraft early that year. In an attempt to raise circulation, he had enlisted the services of escape artist Harry Houdini, and he came up with the idea of having Lovecraft collaborate with Houdini on a lightly fictionalized account of an adventure Houdini had had some years earlier. This incident supposedly involved Houdini being kidnapped on a pleasure trip to Egypt, thrown bound and gagged down a deep aperture in Campbell's Tomb, and left to find his way out of the labyrinthine pyramid. As Lovecraft conducted research on the matter, he came to the conclusion that this account was entirely fictitious, so he asked Henneberger to let him use his imagination to its farthest limits.

The resulting story, "Under the Pyramids" (published as "Imprisoned with the Pharaohs"), is actually one of Lovecraft's more entertaining narratives, even though

NEW YORK EXILE

parts of it read like a travelogue. In the end, Houdini, narrating the story in the first person, tells of encountering loathsome hybrid entities in the depths of the pyramid: "*Hippopotami should not have human hands and carry torches . . . men should not have the heads of crocodiles . . .*" But this is only the prologue to the true horror, where Houdini later comes upon a titanic entity that is the original of the fabled Sphinx.

Lovecraft, however, lost the typescript at the Providence train station when he boarded the train to New York on March 2. He had the handwritten manuscript with him, so he and Sonia had to spend the first several nights of their honeymoon in Philadelphia at a stenographer's office retyping the story. Sonia dryly notes that, after the first night, they were "too tired and exhausted for honeymooning or anything else."

This is, obviously, a tactful way of saying that she and Lovecraft did not have sex that first night. Sonia talks frankly about her sexual life with her husband both in her 1948 memoir and in an interview she gave in 1971. She says

LEFT: *A poster depicting escape artist Harry Houdini, for whom Lovecraft ghostwrote "Under the Pyramids." It was sold as a true story, but Lovecraft invented a great deal of it.*

H. P. LOVECRAFT

84

> "HIPPOPOTAMI SHOULD NOT HAVE HUMAN HANDS AND CARRY TORCHES . . . MEN SHOULD NOT HAVE THE HEADS OF CROCODILES . . ."
> ~"Under the Pyramids"

that Lovecraft was a virgin when he married her, that he had read several books about sex before they were married, and that she had to initiate sexual activity every single time over the next two years; the closest he could come to stimulating her was to grab her little finger with his own and tug it while saying, "Umph!" Move over, Casanova! Sonia goes on to say that Lovecraft did not like to discuss sex and became visibly upset at the mere mention of the word.

In the short term, Lovecraft and Sonia had a household to set up. He moved into her spacious apartment at 259 Parkside Avenue, in the Flatbush section of Brooklyn, asking Aunt Lillian to send various papers and effects that he would need for work. He actually wanted Lillian, and perhaps Aunt Annie also, to live with them, but both aunts quickly discounted this suggestion.

Lovecraft was becoming more involved with *Weird Tales* than he wished. In mid-March 1924 he received an offer from Henneberger to become the new editor of the magazine, as the previous editor, Edwin Baird, had been fired. This would have required Lovecraft to move to Chicago, where the magazine's editorial and business office was located. After pondering the matter for some time, he declined.

Lovecraft has been criticized for doing so, but he probably made the right decision. Some have believed that Lovecraft did not want to go to Chicago simply because it had no colonial antiquities, but there were far more serious reasons than that. Having just gotten married and moved abruptly from Providence to New York, he did not wish to uproot himself again, and there was no guarantee that Sonia would wish to come with him or could find work there. Even more significantly, *Weird Tales* was $40,000 in debt, and it was not clear that the magazine would be able to continue publication; if it folded, Lovecraft might have been stranded in Chicago. His fastidious taste might also have led him to fill the magazine with material that was not popular with readers, thereby hastening its demise.

In the end, Farnsworth Wright, who had been appointed interim editor after Baird's dismissal, became the permanent editor of *Weird Tales*, staying on until his death in 1940. It is undeniable that the magazine is largely the creation of Wright, who not only promoted the work of Lovecraft but also of Frank Belknap Long, Clark Ashton

LEFT: *A silhouette of Lovecraft drawn by Perry at Coney Island on March 29, 1925.*

Smith, Robert E. Howard, Henry S. Whitehead, August Derleth, and many other now-famous contributors. At the same time, Lovecraft accused Wright—not always justly—of idiosyncrasy in regard to his own submissions, and several of Wright's rejections of Lovecraft's tales caused him much anguish and shattered his self-esteem as a writer.

The first few months of Lovecraft's and Sonia's marriage appear to have gone well enough. The couple felt prosperous enough to purchase a plot of land in Bryn Mawr Park, a development in Yonkers north of New York City, where they planned to build a house. But then, in August, Lovecraft wrote to his aunts that there was "something of a shortage in the exchequer."

It turns out that Sonia had lost her position at Ferle Heller as early as February 1924, before the couple married. The exact sequence of events is murky, but what seems to have happened is that she was either fired or (more likely) quit her job and attempted to establish her own hat shop. This seems like a very risky move: at a time when nearly every man and woman wore a hat in public, the competition among milliners was fierce (there were at least 1,200 milliners in Manhattan alone in 1924), and Sonia's shop apparently folded quickly, resulting in a significant loss of her savings.

It was only at this time that Lovecraft himself was forced to seek a job—any job—to bring in some income. When he had first come to New York, Sonia had put him in touch with a woman named Gertrude Tucker, who ran a literary agency called the Reading Lamp. Tucker attempted to market some of Lovecraft's writings, but with no success. Lovecraft had to find a job on his own initiative. On August 10 he took out a long ad in the *New York Times* advertising his skills as a "writer and reviser," but it is not clear that anything came of this. He also wrote a long, ponderous letter full of antiquated language and feeble attempts at humor, offering his services as editor or proofreader, which he sent around to a number of magazines and book publishers, but nothing came of this either. On each attempt, Lovecraft found that not having any previous employment record caused potential employers to regard him as a dubious prospect, in spite of his undoubted skills and desire for work.

Now began the futile and humiliating task of seeking jobs outside the realm of literature and publishing, a task that seemed doomed to failure at the start. One of the

> "THAT DAY WAS ONE OF GLOOM AND NERVES—MORE ADVERTISEMENT ANSWERING, WHICH HAS BECOME SUCH A PSYCHOLOGICAL STRAIN THAT I ALMOST FALL UNCONSCIOUS OVER IT!"
>
> –H. P. Lovecraft

most grotesque incidents was Lovecraft's attempt to find a position with a company advertising its services as a bill-collection agency. Lovecraft knew that this position required a salesman who was pushy almost to the point of rudeness, and that he himself was temperamentally unsuited for the job. Another absurdity was an attempt to secure a job with the lamp-testing department of an electrical laboratory.

The aggravation and depression brought on by his unsuccessful job-hunting forays are poignantly indicated in a letter to Lillian: "That day was one of gloom and nerves–more advertisement answering, which has become such a psychological strain that I almost fall unconscious over it!"

Sonia, for her part, was not doing well either. She was employed for a few weeks here and there, but overall she was in the same position as her husband. Then, in mid-October, her health gave way. She had gastric spasms that required her to spend eleven days at Brooklyn Hospital, followed by several weeks spent resting at a farm in New Jersey. (Lovecraft took the occasion to explore the colonial antiquities of Philadelphia more thoroughly than he had done on his honeymoon.)

Lovecraft's writing was not prospering. The only story he wrote during that year, after "Under the Pyramids," was "The Shunned House," written in October. This story was inspired by a visit to Elizabeth, New Jersey, where he saw a spooky old house that reminded him of a fine old colonial structure at 135 Benefit Street in Providence. Lovecraft wove a powerful tale of historical horror, interspersing an account of the real history of the Providence house with strange elements, including a nameless monster buried in the basement of the house. This creature is a kind of psychic vampire, influencing the dreams of the house's inhabitants; it is killed, not by a cross or stake, but by hydrochloric acid. Lovecraft had no particular reaction when *Weird Tales* rejected the story, even though this was the first time he had ever been turned down by the magazine. The story lay unpublished for years.

Soon after Sonia returned from New Jersey, she announced a dramatic decision. She would take a job with a department store in the Midwest (first in Cincinnati, then in Cleveland), while Lovecraft remained in New York. On the last day of 1924 he moved into smaller quarters at 169 Clinton Street, in Brooklyn Heights. For the time being the couple would have to resume a long-distance relationship, as Sonia returned to New York for only a few weeks or days at a time over the course of 1925 and early 1926.

Today, Brooklyn Heights is an expensive and desirable neighborhood, but in 1925 it was seedy and run-down. Lovecraft paid only $10 a week for his one-room apartment, and most of the money he had to live on came from his wife and his aunts. He himself apparently stopped looking for work altogether as the months passed, and the few stories he sold to *Weird Tales* did not bring in much. He had to practice extreme economies, especially in food and clothing. Lovecraft made a virtue of necessity by having only two meals a day; given his rudimentary cooking skills, these largely consisted of coffee (with heaps of sugar), doughnuts, and canned food. For several months he did not even have a stove to cook his meals. The end result was that he lost more than fifty pounds in a few months.

Matters were made worse in late May when thieves broke into his apartment and robbed him of nearly all his clothing, especially three of his suits. Lovecraft did not feel comfortable unless he had four suits: two dark and two light, one of each shade for summer wear and winter wear.

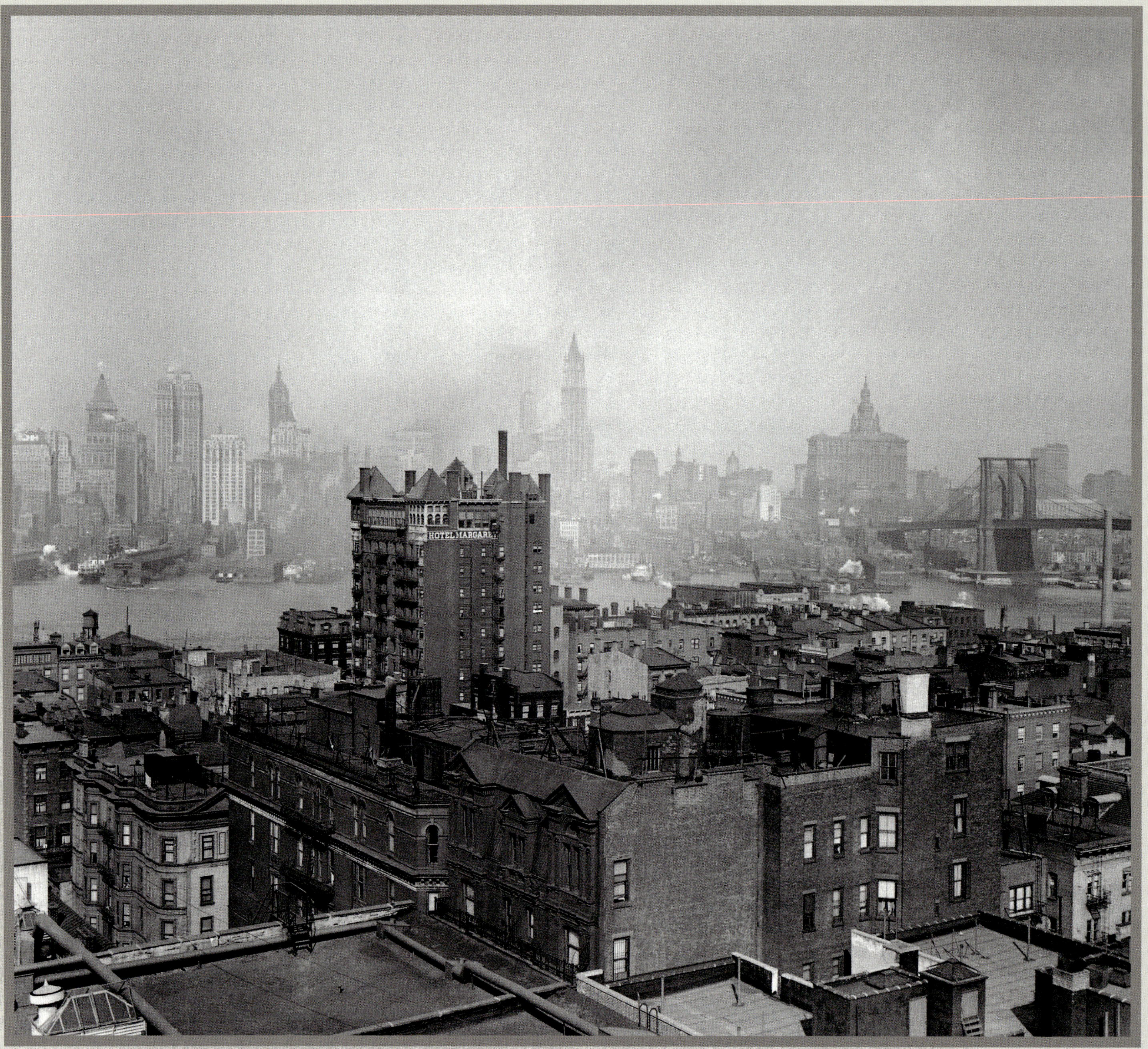

He set out to buy three replacement suits, and for the next several months he wrote obsessively detailed letters to Aunt Lillian about his increasingly shrewd attempts to find bargains across the city.

What saved him, psychologically, was the company of his friends. This was the heyday of the Kalem Club, so named because the last names of nearly all the members began with K, L, or M. Rheinhart Kleiner, Samuel Loveman, and Frank Belknap Long were the core of this group, but others (some of whom Lovecraft had met on his 1922 visits to New York) now joined. There was George Kirk, a bookseller; Arthur Leeds, a kind of rolling stone who tried to eke out a living as a writer; James F. Morton, a Harvard graduate who in 1925 became curator of the Paterson (New Jersey) Museum; and Everett McNeil, an elderly writer of historical novels for boys, who retained a childlike bearing himself while living in Hell's Kitchen, one of the roughest neighborhoods in Manhattan.

Lovecraft came to rely on the support and companionship of his friends, and for much of 1925 he met one or the other of them every single day on various outings or at their homes. So much for Lovecraft the eccentric recluse! He and Kirk established a particularly close relationship as they explored various interesting and out-of-the-way corners of the city. Lovecraft also did some solitary exploration, always on the hunt for colonial antiquities. The modernity of New York had not entirely wiped out traces of its past, and Lovecraft developed a sixth sense in seeking out old relics both in Manhattan and in the outer boroughs.

It is a sad fact that Lovecraft's racism flared up significantly during this period. He had never become used to the ethnic diversity of the city, and he perhaps resented the fact that so many of these immigrants were succeeding in their work whereas he, an Anglo-Saxon of good stock, was in the depths of poverty. Sonia describes him as being "livid with rage" at the mere sight of foreign-born people on the streets. But it is encouraging to note that several friends, especially Frank Belknap Long, have stated that they never saw Lovecraft direct an unkind word toward a member of a minority group.

Lovecraft did relatively little writing during 1925. He produced only three short stories, all in August and September. "The Horror at Red Hook" is one of his

LEFT: *A view over Brooklyn Heights showing the Manhattan skyline, circa 1928.*

most disappointing long tales—a lurid and, in part, racist account of horrors on the underside of the city, focused on Red Hook, an impoverished section of Brooklyn. "He" is a much superior story, and it keenly reflects Lovecraft's despair at being trapped in a city he had come to hate:

> My coming to New York had been a mistake; for whereas I had looked for poignant wonder and inspiration in the teeming labyrinths of ancient streets that twist endlessly from forgotten courts and squares and waterfronts to courts and squares and waterfronts equally forgotten, and in the Cyclopean modern towers and pinnacles that rise blackly Babylonian under waning moons, I had found instead only a sense of horror and oppression which threatened to master, paralyse, and annihilate me.

Lovecraft's final story of 1925, "In the Vault," is another of his most disappointing—a simple supernatural revenge tale in which an embittered old man comes back from the dead to avenge the mutilation of his corpse by a careless undertaker. The idea was suggested by his old amateur friend, Charles W. Smith, editor of the *Tryout*.

"Cool Air," written in early 1926, succeeds in capturing the clangor and bustle of the metropolis, as the narrator finds horror in broad daylight in a decrepit tenement in Manhattan: a Spanish physician, Doctor Muñoz, has perpetuated his life for eighteen years beyond his death by artificial preservation, but the breakdown of his air conditioning unit causes him to collapse in a "dark, slimy trail."

Surprisingly, both "In the Vault" and "Cool Air" were rejected by Farnsworth Wright of *Weird Tales*. In both cases, Wright was apparently thinking of a bizarre legal matter that had occurred a year or two earlier, when the huge May-June-July 1924 issue of *Weird Tales* published a story entitled "The Loved Dead" by C. M. Eddy Jr. This was one of four stories that Lovecraft had revised for Eddy, a Providence friend, and its surprisingly frank account of a man who engages in sex with corpses caused the magazine to be temporarily banned in the state of Indiana. For years Wright was hesitant to accept stories that contained explicit gruesomeness.

One of the things that allowed Lovecraft to bring some order out of the chaos of his life was the request by his friend W. Paul Cook to write a history of horror fiction for publication in his planned amateur magazine, the *Recluse*. Lovecraft plunged into the work in late 1925, finding a renewed sense of purpose in reading the classics of horror fiction and writing about them in a treatise he called "Supernatural Horror in Literature." This thirty-thousand-word essay is not only a sound historical treatment of the subject but an invaluable key to Lovecraft's own predilections in weird fiction.

As the months passed, Lovecraft seemed to be lapsing increasingly into despair and depression. To trace the depths of his feelings as he lived alone in his Brooklyn apartment, one must read a letter he wrote in August 1925 to Aunt Lillian. She had apparently chided him for clinging to his possessions, and Lovecraft shot back:

> It so happens that I am unable to take pleasure or interest in anything but a mental re-creation of other and better days . . . so in order to avoid the madness which leads to violence and suicide I must cling to the few shreds of old days and old ways which are left to me. . . . When they go, I shall go, for they are all that make it possible for me to open my eyes in the morning or look forward to another day of consciousness without screaming in sheer desperation and pounding the walls and floor in a frenzied clamour to be waked up out of the nightmare of "reality" and my own room in Providence.

This is a truly shocking letter for someone to have written to a close relative. The entire letter must be read to gauge how true was Lovecraft's statement in "He" that "my coming to New York was a mistake"–a statement that now carries the added implication that his marriage to Sonia was as well. Would he be compelled to drag out the remainder of his life in a city he loathed, far from the sites of his beloved childhood memories and seemingly unable to earn a decent living? A temporary job in March 1926 as an envelope addresser involved just the kind of mechanical drudgery he found intolerable, but he felt he had no option but to take it. Later that same month, however, at this very lowest point in his New York career, his fortunes turned radically for the better. In short, his aunts had invited him back to Providence.

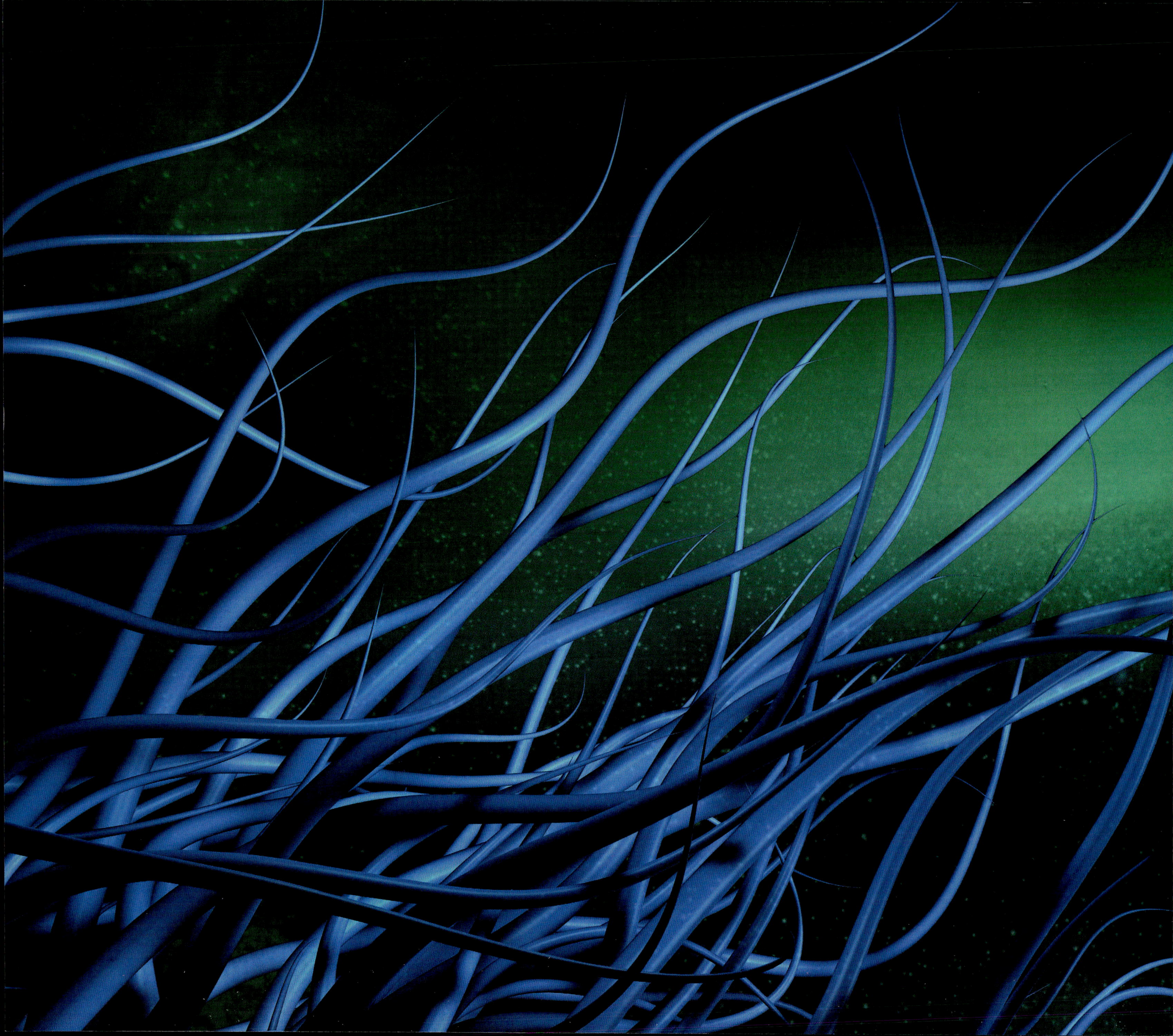

5

THE CREATION OF CTHULHU

(1926–1931)

Exactly why Lovecraft needed an explicit invitation from his aunts to return to Providence is not clear. The matter is discussed in several letters in late 1925 and early 1926, and Lovecraft suggests that Sonia fully endorsed such a move. It could hardly have escaped her attention that her husband was profoundly unhappy in New York, but exactly how–or whether–the marriage could be preserved if Lovecraft left the city was never clarified.

In any event, Lovecraft's ecstasy at the mere prospect of returning to his hometown ("Whoopee!! Bang!! 'Rah!! ... Somebody wake me up before the dream becomes so poignant I can't bear to be waked up!") was exceeded by the drama of his actual return, as related in a letter to Frank Belknap Long:

> Well–the train sped on, and I experienced silent convulsions of joy in returning step by step to a waking and tri-dimensional life. New Haven–New London–and then quaint *Mystic*, with its colonial hillside and landlocked cove. Then at last a still subtler magick fill'd the air–nobler roofs and steeples, with the train rushing airily above them on its lofty viaduct–*Westerly*–in His Majesty's Province of RHODE ISLAND AND PROVIDENCE-PLANTATIONS! GOD SAVE THE KING!! Intoxication follow'd ... I fumble with bags and wraps in a desperate effort to appear calm–THEN–a delirious marble dome [of the State House outside the window–a hissing of air brakes–a slackening of speed–surges of ecstasy and dropping of clouds from my eyes and mind–HOME– UNION STATION–*PROVIDENCE!!!!*

W. Paul Cook saw Lovecraft soon after his return– he and Aunt Lillian had found rented quarters at 10 Barnes Street, north of Brown University. Cook wrote: "He was without question the happiest man I ever saw. ... He was so happy he hummed–if he had possessed the necessary apparatus he would have purred." Cook also went on to remark, of Lovecraft's entire New York experience: "He came back to Providence a human being–and what a human being! He had been tried in the fire and came back pure gold." There is a fundamental truth in the comment: the final ten years of Lovecraft's life saw him become not only the revolutionary weird writer we all know, but also a profound thinker and a warm and genial friend.

Sonia came to Providence a few days after Lovecraft, to help him settle in. At some point the couple discussed the future of their marriage, and of their living arrangements, with Aunt Lillian and Aunt Annie. It is not entirely clear when this occurred—it could have been in the days or weeks after Lovecraft came home, or it could have been a year or two later. In any case, Sonia proposed that she move to Providence to set up a hat shop or other business in town. But the aunts opposed the idea. As Sonia puts it: "At this time the aunts gently but firmly informed me that neither they nor Howard could afford to have Howard's wife work for a living in Providence. That was that. I now knew where we all stood. Pride preferred to suffer in silence; both theirs and mine." What this means is that, to Lovecraft's aunts, the shame of having a "tradeswoman" in the family was too harsh a blow to their social standing. They should not necessarily be criticized for this stance: they had spent their entire lives as members of the informal Providence aristocracy, and even now, when they had descended to a "shabby genteel" status, their pride of lineage was too important to be compromised.

ABOVE: *A page from Lovecraft's letter to Lillian D. Clark (March 29, 1926), testifying to his love of Providence: "Providence is part of me–I am Providence..."*

THE CREATION OF CTHULHU

If anyone is to blame, it is Lovecraft himself for so spinelessly acquiescing to his aunts' decision. In spite of his own quasi-aristocratic pretensions, he probably did not share his aunts' views, and yet he did nothing to oppose them or to work out a compromise. It is very likely that he simply wished the marriage to be over—or, at any rate, that he was content to have a long-distance marriage, maintained only through correspondence. Whatever the case, Sonia was effectively removed from Lovecraft's life.

It is not surprising that, in early 1929, Sonia demanded a divorce. Lovecraft had repeatedly put off the matter because, as he put it, "A gentleman does not divorce his wife without cause," and he felt he had no cause. But Sonia was no longer content with a marriage sustained only by letters, and she finally persuaded Lovecraft to agree to her wishes. Because of the restrictive divorce laws of New York State, the proceedings had to occur in Rhode Island, under the charade that Sonia had deserted Lovecraft, when it was obviously the other way around. To cap the absurdity, Lovecraft neglected to sign the final decree, meaning that the divorce was not finalized; since Sonia remarried in 1935, before Lovecraft's death, that marriage was technically bigamous.

It would be easy to conclude that Lovecraft should perhaps never have married at all, but he himself later came to a different conclusion. Rightly perceiving that he and Sonia were not at all alike in their perspectives on life, he maintained that "With a wife of the same temperament as my mother and aunts, I would probably have been able to reconstruct a type of domestic life not unlike that of Angell St. days." Lovecraft also claimed that the reasons for the marriage's failure were "98% financial," and there is some truth to this. If the couple had had a stable income—and, especially, if they had been able to live outside of the city in a suburban environment like Yonkers, as they had intended—they would have escaped many of the features of big-city life that bothered Lovecraft so much. But it was not to be, and in future years Lovecraft was determined to avoid intimate relationships with women.

Once he settled in, Lovecraft experienced a creative outburst such as he never had before or after: in a period of about nine months, he wrote five important stories and two short novels. Clearly his creative juices had dried up in the stifling atmosphere of New York, and his return to Providence unleashed them in an unprecedented manner.

> "THAT CULT WOULD NEVER DIE TILL THE STARS CAME RIGHT AGAIN, AND THE SECRET PRIEST WOULD TAKE GREAT CTHULHU FROM HIS TOMB..."
>
> ~"The Call of Cthulhu"

The first work to emerge from his pen was "The Call of Cthulhu," written in the summer of 1926. The seeds of this seminal story date to exactly a year earlier, when he wrote a synopsis and devised its title. Set in Providence, it describes the investigations of a Brown professor, George Gammell Angell, into the cult of a creature named Cthulhu. This cult seems to be scattered across the globe—traces of it can be found in the Louisiana bayou, the snows of Greenland, and elsewhere. Angell learns that, according to his worshippers, Cthulhu is an extraterrestrial entity that came from the stars millions of years ago. He and his minions built the immense stone city of R'lyeh, but it sank to the bottom of the Pacific Ocean, trapping Cthulhu under the waves. The legend says that when "the stars are right," Cthulhu will emerge and reclaim control of the earth. Angell dies under mysterious circumstances, and his nephew, Francis Wayland Thurston, continues the investigation. He comes upon the account of a Norwegian sailor, Gustav Johansen, who had actually encountered Cthulhu in the Pacific: R'lyeh had suddenly risen, but before Cthulhu could escape to wreak havoc over the earth, an earthquake caused R'lyeh to sink again, taking Cthulhu with it.

It is impossible to show in a mere synopsis the extraordinary richness of "The Call of Cthulhu." The story is a quantum leap in quality over even the best of Lovecraft's earlier tales, and it embodies his notions of "cosmicism" more keenly than any tale he had previously written. It is not merely that Cthulhu is physically huge ("A mountain walked or stumbled"); it is that his mere presence, albeit underwater, casts a baleful shadow over the entire human race. It is this that Thurston ponders when he writes poignantly at the end: "I have looked upon all that the universe has to hold of horror, and even the skies of spring and the flowers of summer must ever afterward be poison to me."

What exactly inspired the name "Cthulhu" is unknown; Lovecraft says in a later letter, "My rather careful devising of this name was a sort of protest against the silly and childish habit of most weird and science fiction writers, of having *utterly non-human entities* use a nomenclature *of thoroughly human character*; as if alien-organed beings could possibly have languages based on *human* vocal organs." In another letter Lovecraft provides the definitive pronunciation of the name Cthulhu: "The actual sound—as nearly as human organs could imitate it or human letters record it—may be taken as something like *Khlul'-hloo*, with the first syllable pronounced gutturally and very thickly. The *u* is about like that in *full*; and the first syllable is not unlike *klul* in sound, hence the *h* represents the guttural thickness."

"The Call of Cthulhu" is, of course, the first tale that can be considered a full-fledged contribution to the Cthulhu Mythos. That term was not created by Lovecraft—he tended to refer to the pseudomythology he had devised as "Cthulhuism" or "Yog-Sothothery"—but by August Derleth, shortly after Lovecraft's death. The Cthulhu Mythos rests upon the idea that vast creatures from the depths of space have, at various times in history, come to the earth and, more or less by accident, encountered random human beings who cross their path. These creatures include Azathoth, a "monstrous nuclear chaos beyond angled space" who "blasphemes and bubbles at the centre of all infinity"; Yog-Sothoth, who appears as a series of iridescent bubbles or as a creature with ropy tentacles; Shub-Niggurath, a fertility figure who is called "the Black Goat of the Woods with a Thousand Young"; Nyarlathotep, a shape-changer who sometimes takes the form of a suave pharaoh; and Cthulhu, who actually seems to be a relatively minor entity, at least in terms of his power or influence.

Lovecraft pointedly stated that it was from Lord Dunsany that he derived his "artificial pantheon and myth-background." By this he meant that Dunsany, in *The*

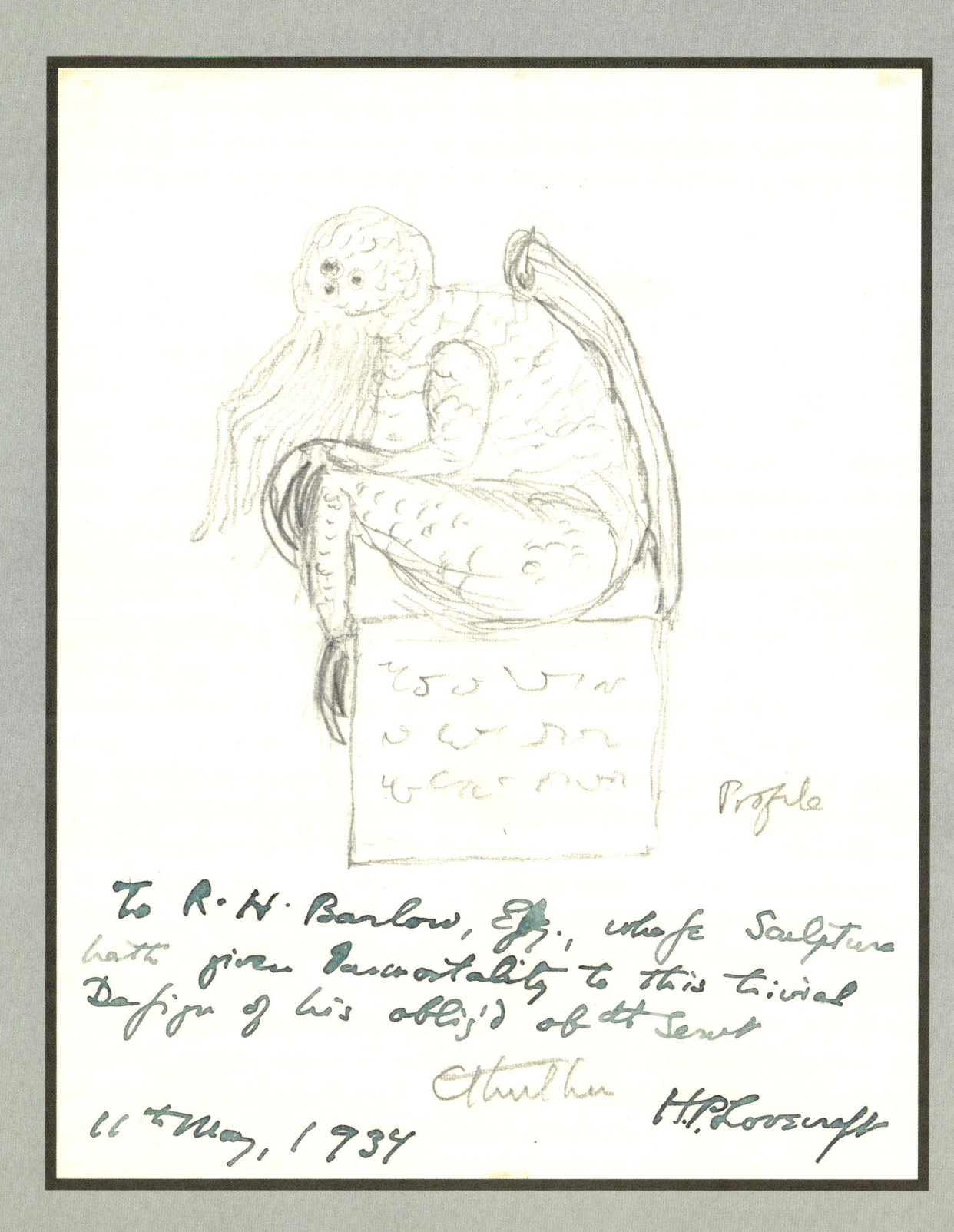

ABOVE: *Lovecraft's own drawing of Henry Anthony Wilcox's dream-sculpture of Cthulhu, dated 1934.*

The tips of the wings touched the back edge of the block, the seat occupied the centre, whilst the long, curved claws of the doubled-up, crouching hind legs gripped the front edge and extended a quarter of the way down towards the bottom of the pedestal.

The cephalopod head was bent forward, so that the ends of the facial feelers brushed the backs of huge fore paws which clasped the croucher's elevated knees. The aspect of the whole was abnormally life-like, and the more subtly fearful because its source was so totally unknown.

—"THE CALL OF CTHULHU,"
H. P. LOVECRAFT

Gods of Pegāna (1905) and Time and the Gods (1906), had invented his own synthetic mythology of gods, demigods, and worshippers; but because he placed these figures in a never-never land of pure fantasy, the element of terror was not uppermost. Lovecraft repositioned his "gods" in the real world, and as a result they are very much a source of terror and dread.

Many readers have wondered how such a fervent atheist could create so many new "gods." These creatures are, indeed, worshipped as gods by certain human cultists, but it is evident that most of them are merely extraterrestrials from remote corners of the universe. They are "godlike" only in terms of their immensity and power. Azathoth is largely a symbol for the inscrutability of an infinite cosmos, and the other entities also have various symbolic functions.

Lovecraft devised various "forbidden books" that contained information about the "gods" and other elements of the Cthulhu Mythos. Chief among these was the Necronomicon of the mad Arab Abdul Alhazred. Alhazred, unearthed from Lovecraft's childhood Arabian Nights phase, was first cited as a "mad poet" in "The Nameless City" (1921), and he became the author of the Necronomicon in "The Hound" (1922). Lovecraft and his friends had great fun in future years in creating more and more books of occult lore, but the matter was not entirely frivolous: to one who had put off suicide as a boy because he wanted to pry out of books the answers to the mysteries of the universe, the idea of a tome containing "forbidden" secrets was very seductive.

Lovecraft outlined his principles for writing "cosmic" fiction in a letter to Farnsworth Wright, written in July 1927:

> Now all my tales are based on the fundamental premise that common human laws and interests and emotions have no validity or significance in the vast cosmos-at-large. To me there is nothing but puerility in a tale in which the human form—and the local human passions and conditions and standards—are depicted as native to other worlds or other universes. To achieve the essence of real externality, whether of time or space or dimension, one must forget that such things as organic life, good and evil, love and hate, and all such local attributes of a

> **"COMMON HUMAN LAWS AND INTERESTS AND EMOTIONS HAVE NO VALIDITY OR SIGNIFICANCE IN THE VAST COSMOS-AT-LARGE."**
>
> ~H. P. Lovecraft

negligible and temporary race called mankind, have any existence at all.

This is an immensely important statement, for it testifies that Lovecraft felt obligated to avoid the standard motifs of supernatural fiction–the ghost, the vampire, the werewolf, the sorcerer, the haunted house, and so on–because they had simply become too implausible in the wake of advancing human knowledge. Lovecraft's monsters had to be original creations that did not rely on outmoded myth or folklore–and their origin in outer space was inevitable, given his "cosmic" outlook. This is why Fritz Leiber referred to Lovecraft as the "Copernicus of the horror story," because he "altered the focus of supernatural dread from man and his little world and his gods, to the stars and the black and unplumbed gulfs of intergalactic space."

A final component of the Mythos was Lovecraft's fictional New England landscape. Although this element does not directly foster the cosmicism that is central to the Mythos, it facilitates it in other ways. What Lovecraft had come to realize, in the two years of what he came to call his "New York exile," was how deeply and irrevocably he was a scion of Providence and New England. He may have taken his cultural heritage for granted before, but when he was uprooted from it and thrust into a very different landscape, he understood how important it was to him. Indeed, it became a kind of emotional bulwark to ward off the feelings of nihilism and despair that might have come from his "cosmic" attitude, which saw the entire human race as insignificant in the boundless expanse of the universe. As a result, Lovecraft spent the final decade of his life not only exploring New England with increasing fervency, but fashioning his own imaginary New England, based on actual history and topography but slyly introducing weird elements along the way. In this way, the landscape serves as the springboard for ever more powerful imaginative voyages to the farthest depths of the cosmos.

Lovecraft wasted no time in putting his newfound devotion to New England to fictional use, as three stories written in the fall of 1926 attest. "The Silver Key," which takes place in rural Massachusetts, and "The Strange High House in the Mist," set in the cliffs of Magnolia, are both endowed with an atmosphere of dreamlike poignancy created by their respective locales. "Pickman's Model," about a Boston artist whose paintings of monsters have an all too real source, is notable for introducing Lovecraft's rubbery, doglike ghouls into his fiction.

These stories set the stage for *The Dream-Quest of Unknown Kadath* (1926–27), a long, meandering short novel about the attempt by Randolph Carter to find a "sunset city" that he frequently dreams about. He searches all through dreamland, finding many other curious entities along the way (gugs, ghasts, zoogs, moonbeasts, even a band of cats, upon whose backs he floats from the moon back to earth), but cannot come upon his sunset city. Finally, in an encounter with Nyarlathotep in a remote and forbidding castle, he learns the truth, as the god tells him:

> For know you, that your gold and marble city of wonder is only the sum of what you have seen and loved in youth. It is the glory of Boston's hillside roofs and western windows aflame with sunset; of the flower-fragrant Common and the great dome on the hill and the tangle of gables and chimneys in the violet valley where the many-bridged Charles flows drowsily. These things you saw, Randolph Carter, when your nurse first wheeled you out in the springtime, and they will be the last

RIGHT: *An aerial view of Boston in the early twentieth century. In* The Dream-Quest of Unknown Kadath, *the main character learns that the mystical "city of wonder" that he has been searching for is none other than his hometown of Boston.*

things you will ever see with eyes of memory and of love.

So all that Carter has to do is to wake up in his Boston home, and he will find the sunset city that he searched for all through dreamland.

Almost immediately after finishing the *Dream-Quest* in late January 1927, Lovecraft undertook yet another short novel, *The Case of Charles Dexter Ward*, finishing it on March 1. At fifty-one thousand words, it was the longest work of fiction he ever wrote; it is unfortunate that, like the *Dream-Quest*, it remained unpublished in his lifetime. Set very much in the real world of Providence, it tells of how the young antiquarian Charles Dexter Ward finds traces of a mysterious and shunned ancestor, Joseph Curwen, who seemed to live to a great age in the eighteenth century until he was killed in a mysterious fashion in 1771. It turns out that Curwen and his associates had mastered the ability of resurrecting the dead through the manipulation of their "essential salts," and in this manner they hoped to probe the minds of the great thinkers of the past to learn the secrets of the universe. Ward resurrects Curwen himself through his essential salts, but Curwen then kills Ward and tries to pass himself off as his descendant. But a valiant physician, Marinus Bicknell Willett, foils Curwen's plans for further depredations.

The Case of Charles Dexter Ward is Lovecraft's greatest tribute to the old-time Gothic mode, but it is also his paean to his hometown. Ward's return from a long trip overseas exactly matches Lovecraft's own return to Providence from New York. Providence is more than a mere backdrop to the events of the tale; it becomes a kind of character in its own right, and Lovecraft is careful to eliminate the horror of Curwen and his cohorts so that his city can emerge pure and unstained.

"The Colour out of Space," written in March 1927, is a very different proposition. Whereas *Charles Dexter Ward* is backward-looking, "Colour" is forward-looking—or, more precisely, outward-looking—and is virtually a tale of science fiction. A meteorite lands on Nahum Gardner's farm in central Massachusetts, far west of Arkham, and its effects are insidious: animals develop strange mutations, fruit and vegetables planted nearby taste funny, and finally the Gardner family itself is affected, first going gradually insane and then, horrifyingly, crumbling to gray dust. This exquisitely modulated tale is one of Lovecraft's great triumphs, precisely because it is impossible to specify exactly what kind of creature (or creatures) emerged from that meteorite and what their goals and purposes are.

It is no surprise that "The Colour out of Space" sold readily to *Amazing Stories*, appearing in the September 1927 issue. This magazine, founded a year earlier by Hugo Gernsback, is regarded as the first science fiction magazine ever published. But Lovecraft refused to submit anything further to it when Gernsback paid him a paltry $25 (one-fifth of a cent a word) for the story.

Lovecraft's views of science fiction were mixed, as can be seen in the later essay "Some Notes on Interplanetary Fiction" (1934), where he states bluntly that "insincerity, conventionality, triteness, artificiality, false emotion, and puerile extravagance reign triumphant throughout this overcrowded genre." Still, he enjoyed the proto-science fiction of Jules Verne and H. G. Wells. More significantly, his own evolving views of weird fiction as something that must be justified by an appeal to science led him inexorably, over the last decade of his life, toward a fusion of the supernatural with science fiction. It is no surprise that two of his most significant tales, At the Mountains of Madness and "The Shadow out of Time," appeared in the science fiction pulp magazine Astounding Stories.

Lovecraft spent much of the rest of his life working hard on writing, revision, and other indoor activities during fall, winter, and spring, and taking long trips in summer up and down the East Coast, from Quebec to Key West, in search of antiquarian relics. These travels became his chief recreational outlet, and he pursued them with a passion. His ever-increasing poverty forced him into incredible economies. Often he would take long bus rides at night to save on hotel expenses; when he did stay overnight, he generally lodged at the YMCA, where he could get a room for a dollar a night. He ate sparingly, relying on packaged goods, and he learned to save expenses by washing his own collars (he still wore old-fashioned detachable collars) and pressing his pants by the tried-and-true method of placing

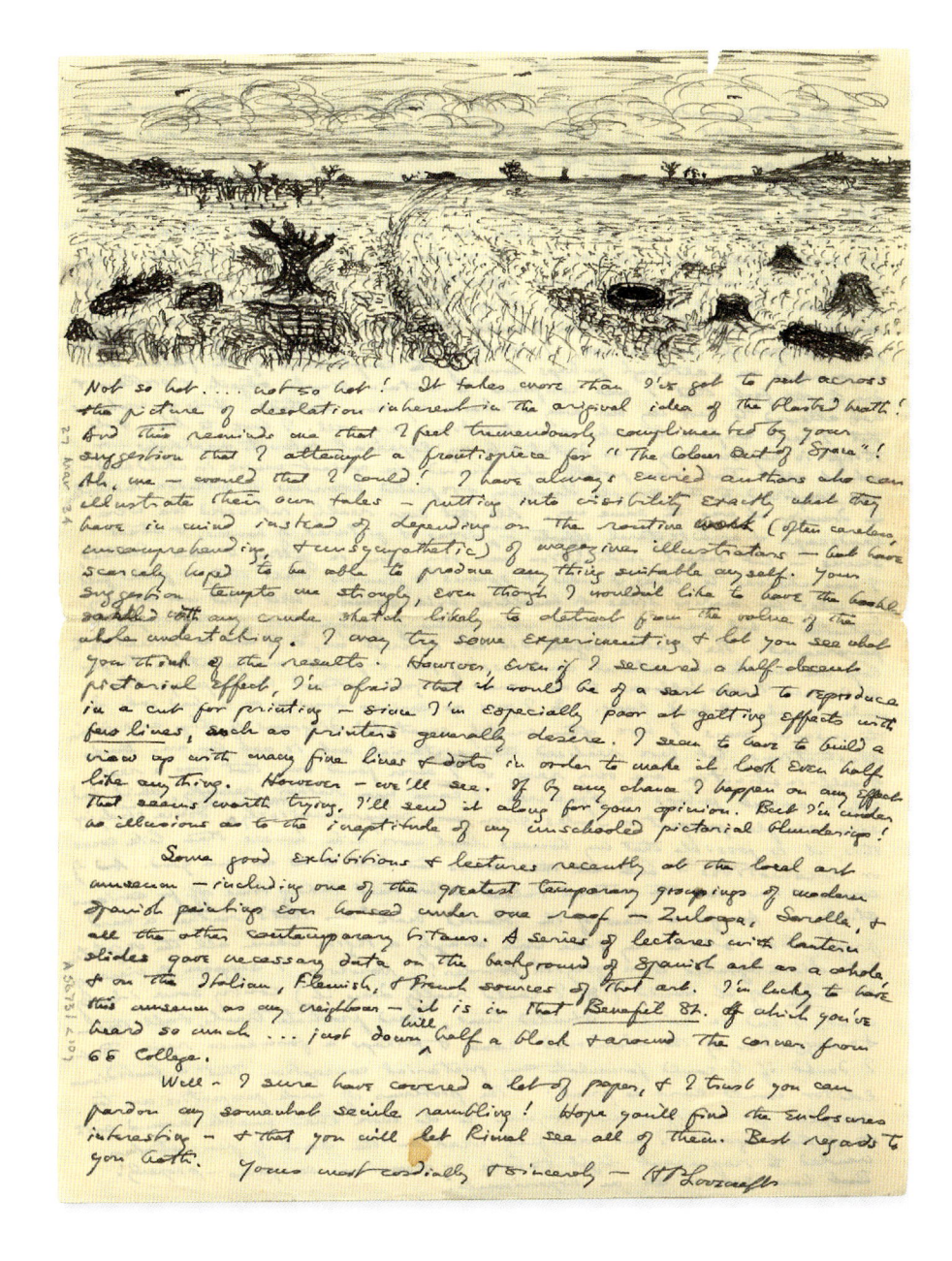

ABOVE: *A page from Lovecraft's letter to F. Lee Baldwin (March 27, 1934), showing Lovecraft's drawing of the "blasted heath" from "The Colour out of Space."*

them between the mattress and box spring when he slept. He even learned to cut his own hair.

These travels were, psychologically, immensely important to Lovecraft. Now assured of a stable base of operations in Providence, he needed the intellectual and aesthetic stimulus of new scenes to rejuvenate his imagination. Many of the locales he visited eventually found their way into his fiction. More than just literary fodder, these trips revived him spiritually, because they reinforced his devotion to an older and (in his view) sounder life and culture. This does not mean that Lovecraft became an antiquated fossil, as he perhaps was in his earlier years; as later events will show, he diligently kept up on current events. But he also believed that contemporary America, with its reliance on speed, machinery, and continual novelty, represented a more intellectually and imaginatively impoverished culture than the eighteenth-century world that he loved.

During the summer of 1927 he took his first trip to Vermont, finding wonder at the unspoiled beauty of the remote rural regions of the state, so different from the comparatively urban environment of southern New England. He also ventured up to Maine. In the summer of 1928 he returned to New York—not by choice, but because Sonia had asked him to help her set up a new hat shop in Brooklyn. He stayed in her apartment for six weeks, but we can be sure that they did not resume marital relations. Indeed, she complains in her memoir that he spent so much time with his friends that she scarcely saw him. Afterward, he ventured up to Vermont again, then to central Massachusetts, where he stayed with an amateur colleague, Edith Miniter. He then moved south on an ambitious trip to the Endless Caverns in Virginia.

This trip partially inspired a new tale, "The Dunwich Horror," written that summer. Set largely in the Massachusetts locale where he had stayed with Edith Miniter, it introduces us to the backwoods town of Dunwich, where a dubious family named Whateley appears to be engaged in curious activities. Wilbur Whateley, the huge, goatish-looking offspring of Lavinia Whateley and an unknown father, dies while trying to steal the *Necronomicon* from the Miskatonic University library. This sets off a chain of events that lets loose an invisible monster locked in the

RIGHT: *The Endless Caverns near New Market, Virginia, where Lovecraft traveled in 1928. His extensive travels that year helped to inspire the story "The Dunwich Horror."*

Whateley house, but the valiant librarian of Miskatonic, Henry Armitage, manages to blast the monster into oblivion by uttering some incantations. It turns out that the entity is Wilbur Whateley's twin brother, and their father is Yog-Sothoth.

"The Dunwich Horror" is a popular story, and for many reasons: it is a rousing narrative, with more overt action than is common in many Lovecraft stories. It also contains a lengthy and evocative quotation from the *Necronomicon*, speaking ominously of how the Old Ones exist "not in the spaces we know, but *between* them." The depiction of the hybrid monster, which one local denizen describes as an "octopus, centipede, spider kind o' thing, but they was a haff-shaped man's face on top of it ... only it was yards an' yards acrost," is one of the more vivid images in Lovecraft's work.

But the story is riddled with flaws. Chief among them is a naive good-versus-evil scenario that Lovecraft had

> "OCTOPUS, CENTIPEDE, SPIDER KIND O' THING, BUT THEY WAS A HAFF-SHAPED MAN'S FACE ON TOP OF IT... ONLY IT WAS YARDS AN' YARDS ACROST."
>
> ~"The Dunwich Horror"

explicitly repudiated in his letter to Farnsworth Wright written a year earlier. Here, "good" is represented by Armitage, and "evil" by Whateley and his clan, who are seeking to usher in a group of monsters from another dimension to overwhelm the earth. Armitage utters all manner of pompous condemnations of Whateley's plans ("We have no business calling in such things from outside, and only very wicked people and very wicked cults ever try to"), and his defeat of the Whateleys is almost comical in its pulpishness. What is more, the story is largely a borrowing of the scenario of Arthur Machen's "The Great God Pan," where the mysterious Helen Vaughan, who wreaks havoc among the gentlemen of London society, is the offspring of Pan and a human woman. Not surprisingly, the story readily sold to *Weird Tales*, bringing in $240 and appearing in the April 1929 issue.

Lovecraft was becoming the focal point of an increasing array of like-minded weird-fiction writers, several of whom contacted him through *Weird Tales*. It was in 1926 that August Derleth (a Wisconsin writer who had begun publishing in *Weird Tales* that year at the age of seventeen) and Donald Wandrei (a Minnesota writer of "cosmic" weird and science fiction) first came into correspondence with Lovecraft. In fact, Wandrei hitchhiked all the way from St. Paul to Providence in 1927 to meet his new friend.

Meanwhile, W. Paul Cook, the legendary amateur printer, published the one and only issue of the *Recluse* in the summer of 1927. It contained not only "Supernatural Horror in Literature" but interesting contributions by many other of Lovecraft's friends. In 1928 Cook printed sheets of *The Shunned House*, but health and financial troubles prevented him from binding and distributing the booklet, which would have been the first stand-alone publication of a Lovecraft story.

Some colleagues, both old and new, now began writing tales inspired by Lovecraft's conceptions. In late 1927 Frank Belknap Long wrote a story, "The Space-Eaters," that featured stand-ins for Lovecraft and himself as characters (the two protagonists of the story are named "Howard" and "Frank"). This is a mediocre and implausible story, but another tale, "The Hounds of Tindalos" (*Weird Tales*, March 1929), is much superior, telling of curious creatures who wander through the angles of space to plague those few humans who can sense their presence.

In the late 1920s Clark Ashton Smith, who had up to that time largely been a poet, began writing stories in great quantity. It cannot be said that these tales were actually inspired by Lovecraft, but Smith perhaps saw how successful his friend was at prose narrative and decided to try it himself. Most of Smith's tales are fantasies set in exotic realms, but a few seem derived from concepts found in Lovecraft's tales.

A new colleague, Robert E. Howard, came into contact with Lovecraft in 1930. He had been publishing in *Weird Tales* since 1925, when he was nineteen, and he was curious about Lovecraft's evolving pseudomythology, thinking it a real myth cycle. When he discovered that it was invented, he took to writing some stories—such as "The Black Stone" (*Weird Tales*, November 1931)—that played off Lovecraft's ideas.

Lovecraft also attracted the attention of would-be horror writers who wished to use his revisory services to make a name for themselves. A curious old man, Adolphe de Castro, had actually collaborated with Ambrose Bierce on translating a German work entitled *The Monk and the Hangman's Daughter* (1891). In the 1920s, with interest in Bierce reviving, de Castro sought Lovecraft's help in revising a memoir of Bierce. Lovecraft declined the job because de Castro would not

THE CREATION OF CTHULHU

ABOVE: *Ambrose Bierce, a leading writer of supernatural and psychological horror in the late nineteenth and early twentieth centuries.*

pay him in advance (Frank Belknap Long, who was also working as a revisionist, helped de Castro with the book, published as *Portrait of Ambrose Bierce*, 1929), but he did help de Castro fix up two stories that had been published in the 1890s. These stories—"The Last Test" and "The Electric Executioner"—are among the poorest of Lovecraft's revisions, because both depend upon the conflict of human characters, something that was not one of Lovecraft's literary strengths.

A more promising client was Zealia Bishop, a Kansas City writer who came up with the flimsiest of plot germs that Lovecraft plotted and developed entirely on his own. "The Curse of Yig" (*Weird Tales*, November 1929) is a compact and effective story, set in the Southwest and introducing Yig, a snake-god that took its place in the pantheon of Lovecraft's imagined "gods." Much more impressive is "The Mound," written in late 1929 and early 1930, a twenty-five-thousand-word novella that Lovecraft spun out of a two-sentence synopsis. Lovecraft took Bishop's trite idea of the ghost of a headless Indian woman seen on a mound in Oklahoma and transformed it into a rich and fascinating tale of a man from Coronado's expedition of 1542. The man makes his way under the mound and encounters an entire civilization of quasi-human creatures who have lived there for centuries. It is far and away his most impressive ghostwritten work and can stand comparison to any of his original tales. But it was far too long for its purpose, and it was rejected by *Weird Tales* because of this. It remained unpublished until after Lovecraft's death.

Lovecraft did not write any original fiction for more than one year after finishing "The Dunwich Horror." But in the winter of 1929–30 he unexpectedly returned to poetry, generating several effective weird poems ("The Ancient Track," "The Messenger") before writing, in a single week, the thirty-six-sonnet series *Fungi from Yuggoth*. This exquisitely crafted cycle eschews the quaint archaism of Lovecraft's earlier verse and is likely to have been influenced by the vigorous but meticulously written poetry of Clark Ashton Smith. (The immediate influence on the *Fungi* may have been Donald Wandrei's *Sonnets of the Midnight Hours*, written in 1927.) As a compendium of Lovecraft's weird conceptions, the *Fungi* is difficult to surpass.

More travel was in the offing. In 1929 Lovecraft visited central Massachusetts, New York City, and several notable places in Virginia, particularly Richmond, Norfolk, Fredericksburg, and Jamestown. The next year he made two epic voyages: first to Charleston, South Carolina, which he deemed a veritable southern Providence because of its gorgeous colonial structures and atmosphere of tranquil antiquity; and Quebec, where he stepped on nominally British soil for the first time. So enthused was he that he wrote long travelogues of both cities, full of historical details and recommendations for walking tours. The Quebec travelogue (not published until 1976) was the longest single work he ever wrote.

Lovecraft finally did get to writing fiction, taking several months of 1930 to write "The Whisperer in Darkness." He put to good use his travels to Vermont of 1927 and 1928, writing a haunting twenty-five-thousand-word novella in which a professor at Miskatonic, Albert N. Wilmarth, gets into correspondence with a denizen of the Vermont backwoods named Henry Wentworth Akeley, who tells him fabulous stories of encounters with strange winged creatures he calls "the fungi from Yuggoth." They have come from outer space to mine a certain element they cannot find on their home planet; in addition, they have tremendous technological skills that allow them to extract the brains of human beings and other creatures and take

ABOVE: *A page from Lovecraft's essay "An Account of Charleston" (1930), with drawings of houses in that southern city.*

them on incredible cosmic voyages. Akeley initially exhibits fear of the fungi, battling them with guns and dogs; later he seems to have a change of heart, urging Wilmarth to come up to visit him and see that the fungi are in fact not hostile to human beings. Wilmarth does so, but flees from the place when he overhears a conversation that leads him to believe that the entity he thought was Akeley was not the man at all, but the shape-changer Nyarlathotep.

Once again, the inadequacy of a plot synopsis of this richly textured story is sadly evident. Lovecraft has captured the atmosphere of rural Vermont in a mesmerizing fashion; he has even used parts of his essay "Vermont— A First Impression," but modified them to augment their horrific suggestiveness. He also put to good use the contemporaneous discovery of Pluto, announced on March 14, 1930, a few weeks after he began the story; in the tale Yuggoth is identified with Pluto. The story, in spite of its length, sold readily to *Weird Tales*, which purchased it for $350 (the largest sum Lovecraft ever received for a single story) and ran it in the August 1931 issue.

Lovecraft's next story met a different fate. He began the short novel *At the Mountains of Madness* in early 1931, completing it on March 22. He had been fascinated with

H. P. LOVECRAFT

the Antarctic since boyhood, and this tale exhibits his fascination with that frozen continent. The Miskatonic Antarctic Expedition of 1930–31, led by William Dyer, is on its way to being a tremendous success when a sub-expedition stumbles upon the frozen bodies of a species unknown to humankind—large barrel-shaped creatures that seem half vegetable and half animal. When the sub-expedition suddenly loses contact with the main camp, two members of the expedition, Dyer and a student named Danforth, fly over to the other camp and find it devastated, with men and dogs killed. As they continue their explorations, they come upon an immense stone city that must have been constructed millions of years ago, long before any human beings were in existence. They are forced to the conclusion that the city was built by the barrel-shaped creatures from outer space, which they call the Old Ones. It appears that those frozen bodies of the Old Ones revived in the sunlight and killed the members of the sub-expedition, but—as Dyer and Danforth discover when they study the bas-reliefs in the Old Ones' city, telling in detail of the history of their species—the Old Ones are not the true horrors. They themselves were overwhelmed by a group of entities they had created, the shoggoths, who look like huge amorphous blobs of protoplasmic slime. In one of the most gripping scenes in all weird fiction, Dyer and Danforth encounter a living shoggoth, which pursues them as they run back to their plane.

At the Mountains of Madness is one of Lovecraft's greatest fusions of horror and science fiction, and it embodies his new principles of writing weird fiction, as stated in a letter of 1931: "The time has come when the normal revolt against time, space, and matter must assume a form not overtly incompatible with what is known of reality—when it must be gratified by images forming supplements rather than *contradictions* of the visible and mensurable universe."

It is perhaps no accident that Lovecraft wrote this novel when he did, for he had diligently followed reports of Admiral Richard E. Byrd's Antarctic expedition of 1928–30. The verisimilitude of the tale is enhanced by Lovecraft's detailed references to biology, paleontology, geology, and other sciences. His lifelong devotion to the sciences may not have led to his becoming a professor of astronomy, but it allowed him to be impressively realistic in the portrayal of the frozen expanse of the Antarctic and of the curious hybrid creatures he had imagined.

The length of the story, however, posed a problem for its salability, and Lovecraft was devastated when Farnsworth Wright of *Weird Tales* rejected it that summer. Wright asserted that the story was "too long," "not easily divisible into parts," and "not convincing." That third comment was merely a rubber stamp that Wright used whenever he wanted to reject a story. What Lovecraft could not see was that Wright was in no position to accept a story purely on its artistic merits. In the case of serials, he had to make sure that readers kept buying the installments, which meant that they needed to be fast-moving, action-packed, and filled with identifiable characters. It cannot be said that Lovecraft's slow-moving, atmospheric tale has any of these qualities.

Wright's rejection may have affected Lovecraft more keenly because he met two further rejections at about the same time. G. P. Putnam's Sons had asked to see some of his stories with a view to book publication. This was the first time that a major publisher had solicited work from Lovecraft, and he was understandably excited. But Putnam's turned down the stories, chiefly because they were too explanatory and were too uniformly macabre in mood. Lovecraft admitted the first criticism but discounted the second; nevertheless, the fact that he would not see a book of his stories from a prestigious publisher left him crestfallen.

The other rejection came from Harry Bates, the editor of a new pulp magazine, *Strange Tales*. This magazine paid two cents a word, a substantially higher rate than *Weird Tales*; as such, it posed a serious threat to the latter. If Lovecraft had been able to find in *Strange Tales* a viable second magazine market, he could have used it as leverage with Farnsworth Wright, who might have been more reluctant to reject a Lovecraft tale lest he lose his star contributor altogether. But the four stories that Lovecraft sent to *Strange Tales* were rejected, and in any case, the magazine folded in 1933 after only seven issues.

In spite of these setbacks, Lovecraft, after undertaking an unprecedented series of travels in the summer of 1931—going all the way down to Key West in Florida, then back up to Charleston, Richmond, and New York—managed to write one more story late in the year, the twenty-five-thousand-word novella "The Shadow over Innsmouth." Whereas *At the Mountains of Madness* is a spectacularly

RIGHT: *The cutter* Bear *and members of Admiral Richard E. Byrd's Antarctic expedition. News of the expedition inspired Lovecraft to write* At the Mountains of Madness.

cosmic narrative, this new tale is one of Lovecraft's greatest ventures into regional horror. A young man, Robert Olmstead (he never provides his name in his first-person account, but it is found in Lovecraft's notes for the story), on a tour of New England, hears of a curious town on the North Shore of Massachusetts called Innsmouth. It has a strange history, and some kind of epidemic occurred in 1846 that killed off many of its residents. Its most notable family is the Marsh clan, but odd things are whispered about Captain Obed Marsh's travels to the South Seas.

As Olmstead explores the city, he encounters an old man, Zadok Allen, who tells him the history of the place. Obed Marsh had made an unholy alliance with a species of half-fish, half-frog creatures he had found in the South Seas: they would provide him with gold and fish, and in exchange they would be permitted to mate with the human inhabitants of Innsmouth. The result is a series of hideous hybrid creatures who, when they become sufficiently mutated, will take to the sea and live forever in an underwater city just off the shore. These creatures pursue Olmstead as he tries to flee the city: "And yet I saw them in a limitless stream—flopping, hopping, croaking, bleating—surging inhumanly through the spectral moonlight in a grotesque, malignant saraband of fantastic nightmare."

But even this is not the culmination of the horror. As Olmstead pursues some genealogical researches, he finds that he is himself related to the Marsh family. In the course of time he develops the "Innsmouth look"—the telltale signs of hybridization. But instead of killing himself, he vows to return to Innsmouth and then plunge into the sea, where he will "dwell amidst wonder and glory forever."

The incredibly realistic description of the decaying backwater of Innsmouth is one of Lovecraft's great triumphs, and shows how he put his wide-ranging travels throughout New England to good use. This story was in fact inspired by a trip to Newburyport, then a decrepit coastal town in Massachusetts, but now restored so that it bears little resemblance to what Lovecraft saw in 1931. It is undeniable that there is a racist substratum to the story: the horror that Lovecraft wishes us to feel at the notion of humans interbreeding with fish-frog monsters is a symbol for the "miscegenation" that he abhorred among human races. But this element does not detract from the atmospheric power of the story.

The writing of the story proved difficult for Lovecraft; he wrote three or four drafts before finding the proper style and mood for the narrative. So depressed was he by his recent rejections that he refused to submit the story anywhere, merely showing it to various correspondents in the hope that their praise might bolster his self-esteem. Whether they did so or not is not entirely clear. Lovecraft later found out that August Derleth had surreptitiously submitted "The Shadow over Innsmouth" to Farnsworth Wright, who rejected it largely for the same reasons that he had turned down *At the Mountains of Madness*.

Despite the string of longer works rejected by magazines, the five years after Lovecraft's return from New York constitute the high point of his creative life, and many of the works that we denote when we use the adjective "Lovecraftian" were written during this short but productive period.

RIGHT: *The first page of the handwritten manuscript of* At the Mountains of Madness, *showing Lovecraft's edits.*

12 sections. | At the Mountains of Madness | The ~~illustrations~~ photographs, both ordinary & aerial, will count in my favour, for they are damnably vivid & graphic. Still, they will be doubted because of the great lengths to which clever fakery can be carried. The ink drawings, of course, will be jeered at as obvious

Even division at beginning of part VI – p 42 – where they are entered | By H P Lovecraft

impostures; notwithstanding a strangeness of technique which art experts ought to remark & puzzle over. In the end

I. I am forced into speech because men of science have refused to follow my advice without knowing why. It is wholly against my will that I tell my reasons for opposing the contemplated invasion of the antarctic – with its vast fossil-hunt & its wholesale boring & melting of the ancient ice-cap – & I am the more reluctant because my warning may be in vain. Doubt of the real facts, as I must reveal them, is inevitable; yet if I suppressed what will seem extravagant & incredible there would be nothing left. I must rely on the judgment & standing of the few scientific leaders who have, on the one hand, sufficient independence of thought to weigh my data on its own hideously convincing merits or in the light of certain primordial & highly baffling myth-cycles; & on the other hand, sufficient influence to deter the exploring world in general from any rash & over-ambitious programme in the region of those mountains of madness. It is an unfortunate fact that relatively obscure men like myself & my associates, connected only with a small university, have little chance of making an impression where matters of a wildly bizarre or highly controversial nature are concerned.

It is further against us that we are not, in the strictest sense, specialists in the fields which came primarily to be concerned. As a geologist, my object in leading the Miskatonic University Expedition was wholly that of securing deep-level specimens of rock & soil from various parts of the Antarctic continent, aided by the remarkable drill devised by Prof. Frank H. Pabodie of our engineering department. I had no wish to be a pioneer in any other field than this; but I did hope that the use of this new mechanical appliance at different points along previously explored paths would bring to light materials of a sort hitherto unreached by the ordinary methods of collection. Pabodie's drilling apparatus, as the public knows already from our reports, was unique & radical in its lightness, portability, & capacity to combine the ordinary artesian drill principle with the principle of the small circular rock drill in such a way as to cope quickly with strata of varying hardness. Steel head, jointed rods, gasoline motor, collapsible wooden derrick, dynamiting paraphernalia, cording, rubbish-removal auger, & sectional piping for bores 5 inches wide & 1000 feet deep all formed, with needed accessories, no greater load than three seven-dog sledges could carry; this being made possible by the clever aluminium alloy of which most of the metal objects were fashioned. Four large Dornier planes, with added fuel-warming & quick-starting devices worked out by Pabodie, could transport our entire expedition from a base at the edge of the great ice barrier to various suitable inland points, & from these points a sufficient quota of dogs would serve us. We planned to cover as great an area as one antarctic season – or longer, if absolutely necessary – would permit, operating mostly in the mountain ranges & on the plateau south of Ross Sea; regions explored in varying degree by Shackleton, Amundsen, Scott, & Byrd. With frequent changes of camp, made by aeroplane & involving distances great enough to be of geological significance, we expected to unearth a quite unprecedented amount of material; especially in the pre-Cambrian strata of which so narrow a range of antarctic specimens had previously been secured. We wished also to obtain as great as possible a variety of

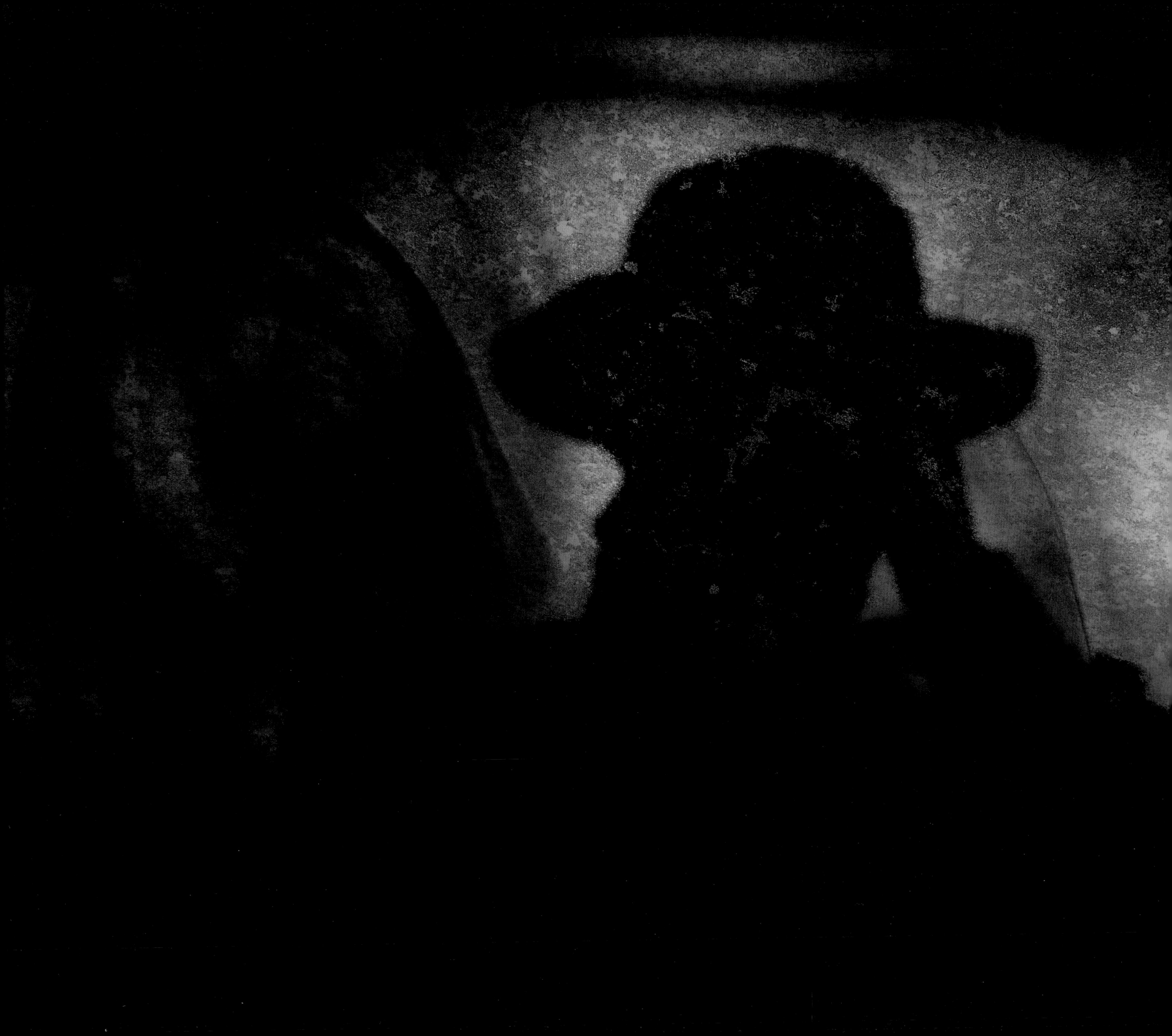

6

A SHADOW OVER LIFE
(1932–1937)

The last five years of Lovecraft's life were beset with creative difficulties, as the psychological effects of rejection plagued him and seemed to dampen his enthusiasm for writing. Indeed, late in life he wrote that the "hostile reception [of *At the Mountains of Madness*] by Wright and others to whom it was shewn probably did more than anything else to end my effective fictional career." However, these final years also saw him undertake travels of unprecedented scope and duration, and they provided him with a sense of renewed aesthetic stimulation that did much to assuage his qualms over what seemed to be a faltering literary career.

Lovecraft did manage to write another story in early 1932, "The Dreams in the Witch House." This novelette might be considered something of a magnificent failure. It deals with a seventeenth-century witch in Arkham named Keziah Mason, who, through knowledge of advanced mathematics, manages to enter into hyperspace and—with her hideous familiar, a ratlike creature with human hands named Brown Jenkin—survives into the twentieth century. A student of mathematics at Miskatonic, Walter Gilman, living in Mason's oddly angled room in Arkham, enters hyperspace in what he believes to be dreams and encounters Mason and Brown Jenkin, who wish to take him to meet Nyarlathotep (disguised in the form of the Black Man of the witch-cult) and Azathoth, "at the centre of ultimate Chaos." Ultimately Gilman is found dead in his room: some ratlike entity has eaten its way through his body to his heart.

The story is in one sense one of the most stupendously cosmic narratives Lovecraft ever wrote, with incredible visions of the fourth dimension (where all entities appear in various exotic geometrical shapes), but overall, the story is clumsily written and conceived, and it is not clear what Mason's purpose is in luring Gilman into hyperspace. Lovecraft deserves credit for his attempt to meld old-time witchcraft with higher mathematics, but the end result is not entirely satisfactory.

Lovecraft, fed up with Wright's rejections, refused to submit the story to *Weird Tales*. But August Derleth, receiving the typescript from Lovecraft, sent in the story on his own initiative, and Wright accepted it for $140.

Lovecraft's 1932 travels constituted another lengthy voyage, starting in New York and proceeding through the South to New Orleans, where he relished the distinctive antiquity of the French Quarter. There he met a new friend, E. Hoffmann Price. Price was a resolutely professional author who tailored his stories for specific pulp fiction markets, regarding writing purely as a business with no artistic overtones. This attitude was anathema to Lovecraft, and the two writers engaged in lively discussions over it in subsequent letters. Price was a dashing and vivid character–Lovecraft describes him as "a war veteran, Arabic student, connoisseur of Oriental rugs, amateur fencing-master, mathematician, dilettante coppersmith and iron worker, chess-champion, pianist, and what not!"–and the two had a splendid time exploring New Orleans.

Lovecraft had to cut his travels short for a sad reason: his aunt Lillian was in the terminal stages of atrophic arthritis, and she died on July 3, 1932. Lovecraft expressed sincere grief at her passing: "The suddenness of the event is both bewildering and merciful–the latter because we cannot yet realise, *subjectively*, that it has actually occurred at all. It would, for example, seem incredibly unnatural to disturb the pillows now arranged for my aunt in the rocker beside my centre-table–her accustomed reading-place each evening."

Lovecraft does not speak often of what Aunt Lillian meant to him, but she must have represented a bastion

ABOVE: *The corner of Dauphine Street and Orleans Street in the French Quarter of New Orleans. This was Lovecraft's favorite part of the city when he visited in 1932.*

A SHADOW OVER LIFE

of stability and one of the last remaining ties to his dead parents. Now, only his younger aunt, Annie, remained of the offspring of Whipple Van Buren Phillips.

Shortly after Lovecraft returned home, E. Hoffmann Price suggested a collaborative venture—a sequel to Lovecraft's story "The Silver Key." Lovecraft did not express much enthusiasm for the task, since the story was a poetic and philosophical narrative that was deeply personal to him. Price nevertheless went ahead and wrote a sequel on his own, entitled "The Lord of Illusion," which he hoped Lovecraft would rewrite. This draft turns the pensive Randolph Carter into a grotesque action-adventure hero who, by the use of the silver key, ventures into the fourth dimension and eventually encounters the archetype of Yog-Sothoth, or something of the sort. Lovecraft correctly recognized that, among many other problems, the tone of the story would have to be significantly altered to match that of the original story.

His eventual rewrite, completed in April 1933 and entitled "Through the Gates of the Silver Key," does not fully reconcile all the difficulties Lovecraft detected in Price's draft; and it adds a further bit of absurdity in having Carter find himself in the body of an alien creature, Zkauba the Wizard, and eventually return to Earth in disguise. Lovecraft retained only a small amount of Price's actual prose, but the overall structure and progression of the story are derived from Price's draft. Farnsworth Wright initially rejected the story, but later accepted it, and it appeared in the July 1934 issue of *Weird Tales*.

Lovecraft was attracting a few additional revision clients who wished to write horror fiction and were drawn to him by his growing reputation. One of the most promising—not because she was a good writer but because she provided Lovecraft with regular work—was Hazel Heald. During 1932–33 Lovecraft revised or ghostwrote a total of five stories for her. None of these can compare with his original tales, but several of them are of some interest. "The Horror in the Museum" (*Weird Tales*, July 1933) is amusing as a parody of Lovecraft's pseudomythology: here we have a museum curator who, on an expedition to Alaska, brings back, not a representation of one of the "gods" of Lovecaft's myth cycle, but *the actual god itself*—an entity named Rhan-Tegoth. And yet, not everyone read the story as a parody, nor were they aware of Lovecraft's involvement, since it appeared only under Heald's byline. Bernard J. Kenton (pseudonym of Jerry Siegel, later the cocreator of Superman) wrote a letter to the *Weird Tales* letter column in which he said: "Even Lovecraft—as powerful and artistic as he is with macabre suggestiveness—could hardly, I suspect, have surpassed the grotesque scene in which the other-dimensional shambler leaps out upon the hero."

"Out of the Aeons" (*Weird Tales*, April 1935) is probably the best of the Heald revisions, and is an interesting fusion of Lovecraft's earlier Dunsanian manner with his myth cycle. Another new "god," Ghatanothoa, is created here—a kind of Medusa figure "whom no living thing could behold . . . without suffering a change more horrible than death itself. Sight of the god, or its image . . . meant paralysis and petrification of a singularly shocking sort, in which the victim was turned to stone and leather on the outside, while the brain within remained perpetually alive."

There is some evidence that Heald took a more than professional interest in Lovecraft. She once invited him to her home in Somerville, Massachusetts, where she prepared a candlelight dinner for him. But Lovecraft was not

RIGHT: *66 College Street, Lovecraft's residence from 1933 to 1937. He moved into an apartment in the building with his last surviving aunt, Annie Gamwell.*

A SHADOW OVER LIFE

ABOVE: *Annie E. P. Gamwell, Lovecraft's maternal aunt.*

much inclined to get dragged into another romance, and we hear little of Heald from this point onward.

In the spring of 1933, Lovecraft saw his ex-wife, Sonia, for the last time. She had invited him to explore some colonial towns in Connecticut, and at the end of the day Sonia said, "Howard, won't you kiss me goodnight?" Lovecraft replied, "No, it is better not to." Not long thereafter, Sonia moved to the West Coast. One day she took all her letters from Lovecraft–and there must have been dozens of them, some extending to fifty pages–and burned them in a field.

It was in the spring of 1933 that Lovecraft and Annie "had a desperate colloquy on family finances," with the result that the two of them decided to form a single household by giving up their two separate apartments and finding one apartment that could fit them both. As luck would have it, a good place soon opened up–an apartment in a house at 66 College Street, owned by Brown University, and costing just $10 a month, equivalent to what each was paying for separate quarters. They moved in on May 15.

Adding to Lovecraft's delight was the fact that the house was built fully in the colonial style. It contained such exquisite touches as a colonial doorway with fan carving and a monitor roof. Lovecraft felt so captivated at finally living in an antique house that for the first few weeks he felt he was living in a museum and would be evicted at closing time. To cap the charm, in the backyard there was a shed on the roof of which the neighborhood cats would sun themselves. Living as he did on Brown's fraternity row, the devoted cat-lover named this band of cats the Kappa Alpha Tau (KAT).

But two distressing events occurred soon after Lovecraft and Annie moved in. Annie fell down the stairs and broke her ankle, causing her to be laid up for weeks, and Lovecraft suffered yet another rejection. This came at the hands of the major publisher Alfred A. Knopf, an editor of which, Allen G. Ullman, had asked to see some stories with a view to book publication. Lovecraft sent in a total of twenty-five stories and crossed his fingers. But he hurt his own cause by disparaging some of the items he submitted; for example, he referred to "The Tomb" as "stiff in diction," "The Temple" as "nothing remarkable," and "The Call of Cthulhu" as "not so bad." No doubt Lovecraft felt he was being gentlemanly and modest in speaking of his work in this manner, but to Ullman he may have come off as lacking confidence in his own work.

The proposed volume was indeed rejected, but not entirely on the merits of the stories. Ullman had asked Farnsworth Wright of *Weird Tales* if he could guarantee the sale of one thousand copies of a book of Lovecraft stories through the magazine. Wright said he could not, and the book was declined. Possibly Wright was being unduly cautious, since Lovecraft was one of the most popular writers of his magazine, but the Depression was in full swing, and the continued existence of *Weird Tales* itself was in doubt—the magazine had had to move to bimonthly publication for a time in 1931.

The Knopf deal was probably the closest that Lovecraft ever came to having a book published in his lifetime by a mainstream publisher. If this had happened, the rest of his career—and, it is not too much to say, the entire subsequent history of American weird fiction—might have been very different. But it was not to be, and Lovecraft had to pick himself up after another humiliating rejection.

Some cheer was lent by the arrival in Providence of the dashing E. Hoffmann Price, who was touring the country by car. On one occasion, he, Lovecraft, and another friend, Harry Brobst, got together to make some chili.

ABOVE: *The first page of the handwritten manuscript of "The Thing on the Doorstep," Lovecraft's tale of a woman who can exchange personalities with her husband.*

Surprisingly, Lovecraft wished it to be as spicy as possible; the three behaved like mad scientists cooking up some nameless and sinister brew. "More chemicals and acids?" Price asked. "Mmm," Lovecraft replied, "this is savory, and by no means lacking in fire, but it could be more vigorous." Brobst, however, made the faux pas of bringing a six-pack of beer. Lovecraft, a lifelong teetotaler, asked in a spirit of scientific inquiry, "What are you going to do with so *much* of it?" Brobst cheerfully replied, "Drink it! Only three bottles apiece." Lovecraft looked at his two friends with some apprehension, wondering if they'd run amok after imbibing so much alcohol.

In a matter of four days in late August, Lovecraft wrote a new story, "The Thing on the Doorstep." This too, like "The Dreams in the Witch House," is a flawed masterpiece. It revolves around Edward Derby, who becomes enthralled with, and eventually marries, a student at Miskatonic University named Asenath Waite, whose family comes from Innsmouth. It becomes evident that Asenath has unusual mental powers–in particular, the power to thrust her mind into the body of another person, whose own mind is then thrown into her own body. This seems to happen regularly with her new husband, and Edward

> "THERE ARE BLACK ZONES OF SHADOW CLOSE TO OUR DAILY PATH, AND NOW AND THEN SOME EVIL SOUL BREAKS A PASSAGE THROUGH."
>
> ~"The Thing on the Doorstep"

appeals to his friend, Daniel Upton, to assist him in ridding himself of his demon wife. In a spectacularly grisly climax, Edward kills Asenath, but her mind remains alive and she emerges from her own body and occupies the body of her husband. Edward, now in the decaying body of his wife, buried in the cellar, manages to dig himself out; he presents himself to Upton's house as "the thing on the doorstep."

The tale is, again, somewhat crudely written, and there is very little suspense or surprise in the overall narrative. Moreover, the basic premise of mind-exchange was taken from two different books that Lovecraft read—Barry Pain's *An Exchange of Souls* (1911) and H. B. Drake's *The Shadowy Thing* (1928). Lovecraft again refused to submit the story anywhere, and it merely circulated among his friends.

It was around this time that Lovecraft began attracting the attention of a number of young fans and writers who looked upon him as a towering figure in pulp fiction. Several of these individuals became leading writers of weird fiction in later years, and others launched what would become known as the fantasy fandom movement. This movement was similar to amateur journalism in the sense that it was largely guided by youngsters (almost all of them boys) who established their own fledgling magazines and published them on their own printing presses;

A SHADOW OVER LIFE

ABOVE: *Lovecraft in De Land, Florida, where he visited his young friend R. H. Barlow in the summers of 1934 and 1935.*

but the focus was exclusively on horror, fantasy, and science fiction.

The first such magazine was the *Fantasy Fan*, which appeared in eighteen monthly issues from September 1933 to February 1935. It was the brainchild of Charles D. Hornig, who was only seventeen at the time the magazine was founded. He solicited the contributions of Lovecraft, Clark Ashton Smith, and even such resolutely professional writers as August Derleth and Robert E. Howard, making his journal a lively forum for the "Lovecraft circle." A less polished figure was William L. Crawford, whose scholastic limitations caused Lovecraft to refer to him unkindly as "Hill-Billy Crawford." Crawford established the short-lived magazines *Marvel Tales* and *Unusual Stories*, the former of which printed several works by Lovecraft.

Among the writers, two stand out. The first is Robert H. Barlow, who began corresponding with Lovecraft in 1931 at the tender age of thirteen. Lovecraft did not know for several years how young Barlow was, only discovering the secret when he spent several weeks with his friend in De Land, Florida, in the summer of 1934. By this time Barlow had begun writing fantasy fiction, more inspired by Lord Dunsany and Clark Ashton Smith than by

Lovecraft or the horror tradition, but Lovecraft found much value in this work. Barlow never established himself as a professional writer, but he was of value to Lovecraft in a very different regard, as we shall see presently.

The other writer is Robert Bloch, the author of *Psycho*, who was sixteen when he began writing to Lovecraft in 1933. Bloch was soon writing horror tales and sending them to Lovecraft to look over. The latter offered him valuable advice on plotting, structure, motivation, and other key elements; in particular, he urged Bloch to tone down the flamboyance of his prose, since he knew that this was a besetting sin of his own early work. Bloch achieved quick success in *Weird Tales*, landing stories there as early as 1935, and in later years he would have a distinguished career in the fields of horror and suspense.

In 1935 and 1936, several other young writers came to his attention. These ranged from Donald A. Wollheim, editor of the fanzine *The Phantagraph* and later a distinguished editor in the science fiction field; Henry Kuttner, a writer of horror and science fiction whom Lovecraft introduced to his future wife, C. L. Moore, also a noted writer; and Fritz Leiber, one of the most heralded authors of horror, fantasy, and science fiction in the succeeding decades. Leiber has testified to the immense benefits of his brief, six-month correspondence with Lovecraft, in which the older writer gave him valuable advice about the craft of writing and encouragement for Leiber's early experiments in both fiction and poetry.

After his two-month visit to Barlow and an ecstatic visit to the island of Nantucket later in the summer, Lovecraft did buckle down to write a story. His first draft was a mere sixteen pages, but he realized that this did not come close to exhausting the artistic possibilities of the scenario; he began a wholesale rewrite, not finishing it until February 22, 1935. He called it "The Shadow out of Time."

Nathaniel Wingate Peaslee, a professor of economics at Miskatonic University, is taken ill in the middle of a lecture in 1908. He seems to be suffering complete amnesia: not only can he not remember who he is, but he has even lost the ability to speak and walk. Over the next five years, he relearns how to live, and displays unusual traits: he absorbs books at a superhuman rate and conducts all manner of expeditions to out-of-the-way regions of the world. Suddenly, in 1913, his memory returns—but he is plagued by strange dreams. These dreams focus on an extraterrestrial

Had I, as the captive mind of those shambling horrors, indeed known that accursed city of stone in its primordial heyday, and wriggled down those familiar corridors in the loathsome shape of my captor? Were those tormenting dreams of more than twenty years the offspring of stark, monstrous *memories*? Had I once veritably talked with minds from reachless corners of time and space, learned the universe's secrets, past and to come, and written the annals of my own world for the metal cases of those titan archives?

–"THE SHADOW OUT OF TIME,"
H. P. LOVECRAFT

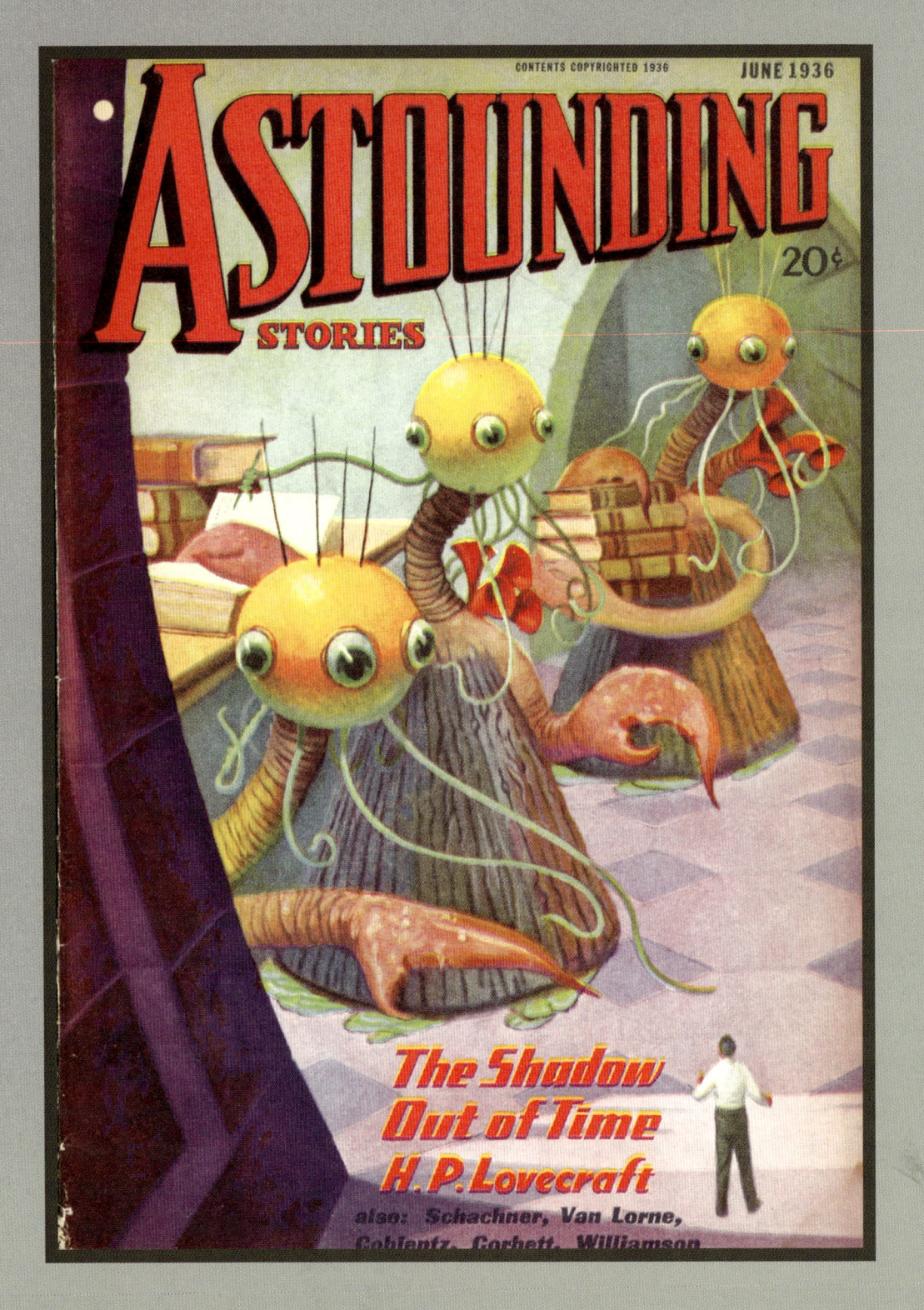

ABOVE: *The cover of* Astounding Stories *(June 1936), featuring Howard Brown's illustration for Lovecraft's story "The Shadow out of Time." It depicts Nathaniel Wingate Peaslee encountering members of the alien Great Race.*

species, the Great Race, who are shaped like ten-foot-high rugose (or wrinkled) cones and who have mastered the ability to exchange minds *over time*—that is, they can swap minds with other entities of both the past and the future. In this way, they have learned all the secrets of the universe. Peaslee dreams that his body was taken over in 1908–13 by a mind from a member of the Great Race; meanwhile, Peaslee's own mind, thrust into the body of his captor, writes a history of his own time for the Great Race's immense archives. All this, Peaslee dreams, took place one hundred and fifty million years ago.

Peaslee passes these dreams off as by-products of his esoteric learning during his amnesia, but he is disturbed when he is contacted by a mining engineer in Australia who has come upon incredibly ancient ruins that seem very similar to those that Peaslee described in articles he had written on the subject. Going to Australia, he is horrified to find his dreams literally coming true. In an incredibly potent climactic scene, Peaslee explores the underground ruins of the Great Race's city, comes upon its archives, and sees the document he must have written millions of years ago.

Just as *At the Mountains of Madness* conveys with unmatched power the immensity of space, so does "The Shadow out of Time" convey the immensity of time. The sense of incalculable eons spanned by the questing minds of the Great Race is one of the imperishable scenarios in weird and science fiction. These two long stories embody the essence of Lovecraft's cosmicism, and, along with "The Colour out of Space," they constitute the pinnacle of his literary achievement.

Even more interestingly, these two tales also reflect a significant shift in Lovecraft's political perspective. In his earlier days he was defiantly reactionary, adhering to monarchism and even fascism (he welcomed Mussolini's takeover of Italy in 1922). But with the onset of the Depression, Lovecraft began thinking more searchingly about the problems of politics and economics. He came to the conclusion that unrestrained capitalism was a cruel and inhumane system and must be replaced by moderate (non-Marxist) socialism, with such elements as unemployment insurance, Social Security, and artificial limitation of working hours so that more people could be employed. After being a lifelong Republican, he voted enthusiastically for Franklin D. Roosevelt in 1932 and 1936; he supported the New Deal and wished FDR to proceed even more boldly with reform.

These concerns are reflected not only in such essays as "Some Repetitions on the Time" (1933) but in his fiction. The Old Ones of *At the Mountains of Madness* and the Great Race of "The Shadow out of Time" embody, in their various ways, the quasi-socialist utopia that Lovecraft envisioned. If even these species, for all their intellectual and technological superiority, eventually went into decline, it was only a natural result of the inevitable rise and fall of civilizations—a concept that Lovecraft had picked up from reading Oswald Spengler's influential treatise *The Decline of the West* (1926–28).

Lovecraft was, however, so dissatisfied with the quality of "The Shadow out of Time" that he refused even to prepare a typescript of it. Instead, he sent the handwritten manuscript—scribbled in an old school composition book—to August Derleth, in the hope that he might have the patience to read through the text and render a positive verdict. It doesn't seem as if Derleth got very far, and the story languished.

Lovecraft's travels in the summer of 1935—the last, as it happened, that he would undertake—focused again on Florida, as R. H. Barlow had invited Lovecraft to stay as long as he wished. Lovecraft arrived in De Land on June 9 and remained until August 18. Among numerous writing and printing projects, Barlow did Lovecraft an immense favor. He had wanted to read "The Shadow out of Time," and Lovecraft asked Derleth to send the manuscript down to Florida. Barlow not only read the story but secretly prepared a typescript of it. Lovecraft—whose phobia of typing had by this time reached almost pathological levels—was overjoyed; but instead of submitting the story to a publisher, he sent it on the rounds of his friends and colleagues.

In September, Lovecraft attended a party in New York where he met the young science fiction fan Julius Schwartz. Schwartz, then only twenty years old, was attempting to establish himself as an agent, and he asked Lovecraft if he had any manuscripts that needed placing. Lovecraft mentioned his science fiction/horror tale of 1931, *At the Mountains of Madness*. Schwartz later obtained the typescript and walked into the office of F. Orlin Tremaine, editor of *Astounding Stories,* which along with *Amazing Stories* was the leading pulp magazine in

RIGHT: *The first page of the handwritten manuscript of "The Shadow out of Time," one of Lovecraft's masterpieces. The manuscript's whereabouts were unknown for nearly fifty years.*

Begun Nov 10, 1934

The Shadow Out of Time
By H P Lovecraft

I.

After 22 years of nightmare & terror, saved only by a desperate conviction of the mythical source of certain impressions, I am unwilling to vouch for the truth of that which I think I found in Western Australia on the night of July 17-18, 1935. There is reason to hope that my experience was wholly or partly an hallucination — for which, indeed, abundant causes existed. And yet, its realism was so hideous that I sometimes find hope impossible. If the thing did happen, then man must be prepared to accept notions of the cosmos, & of his own place in the seething vortex of time, whose merest mention is paralysing. He must, too, be placed on guard against a specific lurking peril which, though it will never engulf the whole race, may impose monstrous & unguessable horrors upon certain venturesome members of it. It is for this latter reason that I urge, with all the force of my being, a final abandonment of all attempts at unearthing those fragments of unknown, primordial masonry which my expedition set out to investigate.

Assuming that I was sane & awake, my experience on that night was such as has befallen no man before. It was, moreover, a frightful confirmation of all I had sought to dismiss as myth & dream. Mercifully there is no proof, for in my fright I lost the awesome object which would — if real & brought out of that noxious abyss — have formed irrefragable evidence. When I came upon the horror I was alone — & I have up to now told no one about it. I could not stop the others from digging in its direction, but chance & the shifting sand saved them from finding it. Now I must formulate some definitive statement — not only for the sake of my own mental balance, but to warn such others as may read it seriously.

These pages — much in whose earlier parts will be familiar to close readers of the general & scientific press — are written in the cabin of the ship that is bringing me home. I shall give them to my son, Prof. Wingate Peaslee of Miskatonic University — the only member of my family who stood by me after my queer amnesia of long ago, & the man best informed on the inner facts of my case. Of all living persons, he is least likely to ridicule what I shall tell of that fateful night. I did not enlighten him orally before sailing, because I think he had better have the revelation in written form. Reading & re-reading at leisure will leave with him a more convincing picture than could my confused tongue convey.

He can do as he thinks best with this account — showing it, with whatever comment he may deem proper, to any quarters where it will be likely to accomplish the effect I desire. It is for the sake of such readers as are unfamiliar with the earlier phases of my case that I am prefacing the revelation itself with a fairly ample summary of its background.

My name is Nathaniel Wingate Peaslee, & those who recall the newspaper tales of a generation back — or the letters & articles in psychological journals six or seven years ago — will know who & what I am. The press was filled with details of my strange amnesia in 1908-13, & much was made of the traditions of horror, madness, & sorcery which lurked behind the ancient Massachusetts town that I choose for my place of residence. Yet I would have it known that there is nothing whatever of the mad or sinister in my heredity & early life. This is a highly important fact in view of the shadow which fell so suddenly upon me from outside sources. It may be that centuries of dark brooding had given to crumbling, whisper-haunted Arkham a peculiar vulnerability as regards such shadows — though even this seems doubtful in the light of those other cases which I later came to study. But the chief point is that my own ancestry & background are altogether

> "I WAS NEVER CLOSER TO THE BREAD-LINE THAN THIS YEAR."
>
> ~H. P. Lovecraft

the science fiction field. Schwartz told Tremaine, "I have in my hands a thirty-five-thousand-word story by H. P. Lovecraft." Tremaine replied: "You'll get a check on Friday." In other words, Tremaine accepted the story without reading it. If nothing else, this testifies to Lovecraft's high reputation in the realm of pulp fiction. Tremaine bought the story for $350; subtracting Schwartz's ten percent commission, this left $315 for Lovecraft.

Hearing about this sale, Donald Wandrei, who had the typescript of "The Shadow out of Time" in his possession, took the story over to Tremaine. Tremaine accepted it, again without reading the story; for this one he paid $280. Wandrei refused to take a commission for his work as informal agent.

Lovecraft was so buoyed up by the double sale that he promptly wrote a new story, "The Haunter of the Dark," in early November. The tale's conception was curious. Robert Bloch had written a story, "The Shambler from the Stars" (*Weird Tales*, September 1935), in which a character transparently based on Lovecraft suffers a hideous end at the hands of a nameless entity. A reader of *Weird Tales* sent a letter to the editor suggesting that Lovecraft repay the favor by writing a story featuring Bloch as a character. Lovecraft did so, writing about the young writer Robert Blake who comes to Providence and becomes fascinated with an abandoned church, in Federal Hill (the city's Italian district) that has a dubious history. Blake unwittingly releases a creature—an avatar of Nyarlathotep—that had been sealed up in the church's belfry. The creature is killed by a stroke of lightning as it is flying out of the church, but because it had already fused its mind with Blake's, Blake himself is killed.

The story is most interesting for its autobiographical touches. The apartment that Blake occupies is an accurate portrayal of Lovecraft's own living quarters at 66 College Street, while the church in question is St. John's Catholic Church, long a fixture in Federal Hill but torn down in recent years. Lovecraft didn't know it, but he had written his last work of original fiction.

The two *Astounding* sales—bringing in $595 in a year when Lovecraft had had no professional fiction sales for the entire year—were a veritable godsend. As he put it poignantly, "I was never closer to the bread-line than this year." Lovecraft claimed that he had managed to reduce his expenses so that he could survive on $15 a week, including food, rent, and other essentials; this meant that the two story sales would have provided his income for some forty weeks.

ABOVE: *Lovecraft on the doorstep of 66 College Street, where he had an apartment with his aunt Annie in the last years of his life.*

A SHADOW OVER LIFE

ABOVE: *Anne Tillery Renshaw, longtime friend and colleague of Lovecraft, with whom he wrote a textbook of English usage.*

But Lovecraft was less happy when he actually saw the stories in print. *At the Mountains of Madness* appeared in the February, March, and April 1936 issues of *Astounding*. Lovecraft was appalled that his long, leisurely paragraphs had been broken up into shorter ones, presumably for easier reading among the half-literate connoisseurs of the pulps; more seriously, a bungling editor had cut down the climactic scene of the encounter with the shoggoths to save a little space, with the result that it reads confusingly and even incoherently. "The Shadow out of Time" appeared in the June 1936 issue; and, although it was not actually abridged, its paragraphs were also broken up.

By this time, however, Lovecraft did not have the luxury to worry about textual niceties. The year 1936 was in nearly every way a disaster for him. He wrote not a single work of original fiction, but found himself bogged down with tempest-in-a-teapot controversies in the NAPA. He was also stunned to hear of the suicide of his correspondent Robert E. Howard on June 11. The work he did accomplish was tedious and unprofitable, helping his amateur colleague Anne Tillery Renshaw with a textbook of English usage. This work, published as *Well Bred Speech* (1936), occupied much of his time during the fall;

on one occasion in late September, he worked for sixty hours without a break to get the book done on time.

To gauge the depths of Lovecraft's poverty at this time, we have only to read an informal diary that he kept in the spring of 1936, when Annie was hospitalized for breast cancer. The severe economies Lovecraft had to practice—which included eating old canned food that had been lying around since the Barnes Street days, as well as a ten-year-old tin of cocoa—make painful reading. The small sums that Lovecraft and Annie had inherited from Whipple Phillips's estate were no doubt nearly exhausted, with little prospect for more revenue beyond what Lovecraft's writing and revision work could bring in.

Only a few months before his death, Lovecraft finally held in his hands a book of his fiction—but the result was far from what he had hoped for. William L. Crawford released "The Shadow over Innsmouth" in November 1936 under the imprint of the Visionary Press. But this small-press venture was a boondoggle from start to finish. The typesetting was so poor that, even after repeated corrections of proofs, the book still contained many errors, and Lovecraft forced Crawford to insert an errata list into each copy. Crawford printed four hundred copies but bound only two hundred in a cheap and shoddy hardcover binding, which he sold for $1; later, the other two hundred copies were destroyed. The book made no real impression, even in the tiny world of fantasy fandom.

By the time the book came out, Lovecraft was not in much of a mood to appreciate its dubious merits. His health had been deteriorating for years. As early as 1934 he spoke of suffering an attack of "grippe" (an old-fashioned term for the flu). In fact, he had developed cancer of the small intestine. It is now difficult to ascertain the exact causes of Lovecraft's ailment, but his poor diet—full of fats and sugars, and with the near-total absence of fruits and vegetables—was surely a major factor.

By the fall of 1936 Lovecraft was becoming increasingly incapacitated, but he never saw a physician. Perhaps his poverty fueled his reluctance, as well as his recollection that his mother had died after a gall bladder operation. In any case, his condition continued to worsen, and a doctor, Cecil Calvert Dustin, was finally brought in on February 16, 1937. Dustin saw immediately that Lovecraft was in the terminal stages of cancer; all that could be done was to relieve his pain if possible.

RHODE ISLAND PUBLIC HEALTH COMMISSION

Division of Vital Statistics

CERTIFICATE OF DEATH

City or Town No. 151

1. **PLACE OF DEATH**
   City or Town: Providence, R. I.   St. and No.: Jane Brown Memorial Hospital
   (If death occurred in a hospital or institution, give its NAME instead of street and number)
   Length of residence in city or town where death occurred: 46 yrs 6 mos 23 ds. How long in U. S. if of foreign birth? ...... yrs ...... mos ...... ds.

2. **FULL NAME**: Howard Phillips Lovecraft   War Record: None *(Name of War)*

   (a) Residence:
   St. and No.: 66 College Street   City or Town: Providence, R. I.
   (If nonresident give city or town and State)   (Usual place of abode)

PERSONAL AND STATISTICAL PARTICULARS	MEDICAL CERTIFICATE OF DEATH
3. SEX: Male 4. COLOR OR RACE: White 5. Single, Married, Widowed, or Divorced: Single	21. DATE OF DEATH: March 15, 1937
5a. If married, widowed, or divorced (if wife, FULL MAIDEN name) HUSBAND (or) WIFE: —	22. I HEREBY CERTIFY, That I attended deceased from Mar 5, 1937, to Mar 15, 1937. I last saw him alive on Mar 14, 1937, death is said to have occurred on the date stated above at 7:15 A.m.
6. DATE OF BIRTH: Aug. 20, 1890	The principal cause of death and related causes of importance were as follows:
6a. If STILLBORN enter that fact here. Months of gestation: —	
7. AGE: 46 Years, 6 Months, 23 Days	Carcinoma of small intestine — Date of onset 1936
8. Trade, profession, or particular kind of work done: Author	
9. Industry or business in which work was done: General Subjects	
10. Date deceased last worked at this occupation: Feb. 1937	Other contributory causes of importance: Chronic nephritis — 1936
11. Total Time (years) spent in this occupation: 26 yrs	
12. BIRTHPLACE: Providence, Rhode Island	
13. FATHER NAME: Winfield S. Lovecraft	Name of operation: None Date of: —
14. BIRTHPLACE: Mount Vernon, New York	Was there an autopsy? No What tests confirmed diagnosis? Blood chemistry, urinalysis
15. MOTHER MAIDEN NAME: Sarah S. Phillips	23. If death was due to external causes (violence) fill in also the following:
16. BIRTHPLACE: Foster, Rhode Island	Accident, suicide, or homicide? —— Date of injury: —, 19— Where did injury occur? —— Specify whether injury occurred in industry, in home, or in public place.
17. INFORMANT: Annie P. Gamwell (Address) 66 College Street (Relation to deceased) Aunt	
18. BURIAL ☒ CREMATION ☐ REMOVAL ☐ or OTHERWISE ☐ City or Town: Providence, R. I. Name of Cemetery: Swan Point Cemetery	Manner of injury: —— Nature of injury: ——
19. Signature of Embalmer: Henry F. Sanderson #215 (License No.) Funeral Director: Horace B. Knowles' Sons R.I.	24. Was disease or injury in any way related to occupation of deceased? No If so, specify: —— (Signed) Wm. Leslie Leet M.D. (Degree) (Address) 199 Thayer St.
20. FILED MAR 16 1937 Local Registrar	

ELF 24433   Dr. William L. Leet, 199 Thayer St.,

On March 1, a specialist in internal medicine, Dr. William Leet, was summoned, but Leet concluded that little could be done. Finally, on March 10, Lovecraft was taken to Jane Brown Memorial Hospital. Two days later Annie Gamwell wrote a letter to Barlow: "The dear fellow grows weaker and weaker—nothing can be retained in his stomach." At one point, more than six quarts of fluid were drained from his stomach. Harry Brobst, a psychiatric nurse, saw him on March 13, exhorting him to remember the ancient philosophers, who faced death with courage and stoicism.

Since the beginning of the year, Lovecraft had been keeping a brief diary, chiefly focusing on his deteriorating medical condition. This diary (which now exists only in excerpts copied down by R. H. Barlow) makes clear the agony Lovecraft was experiencing during this entire period; the entry for March 1 reads simply: "pain—drowse—intense pain—rest—great pain." The last entry is dated March 11, after which time Lovecraft was apparently unable to hold a pen.

Howard Phillips Lovecraft died at 6:45 a.m. on March 15, 1937. Three days later, he was buried in the Phillips family plot at Swan Point Cemetery, next to his mother and father.

ABOVE: *Lovecraft's burial place in the old Phillips family plot at Swan Point Cemetery in northeast Providence.*

LEFT: *Lovecraft's death certificate.*

A SHADOW OVER LIFE

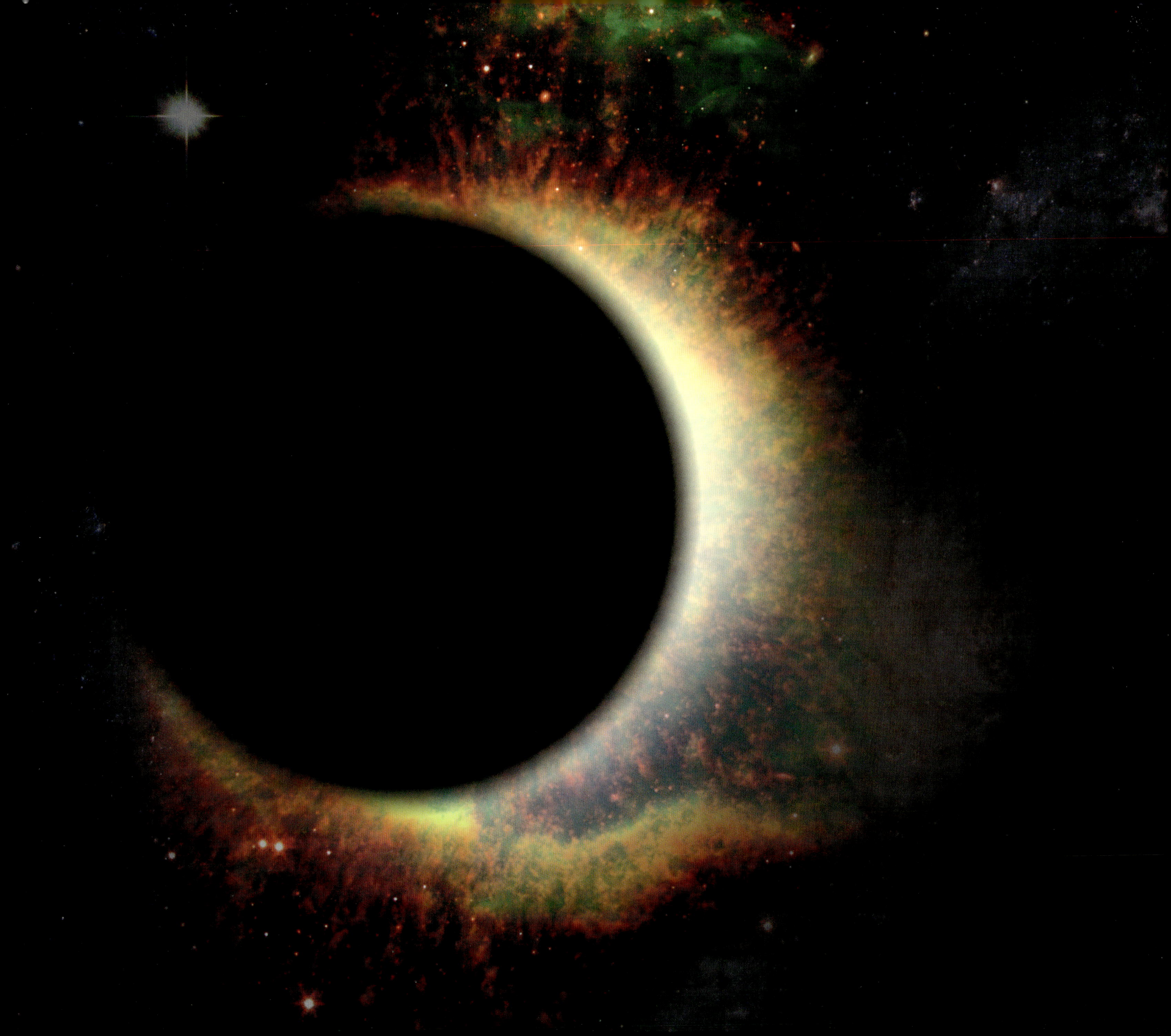

7

THE MYTHOS GROWS

Word of Lovecraft's death spread quickly, aided by a brief notice in the *New York Times*, "Writer Charts Fatal Malady" (March 16), telling of the diary that Lovecraft kept at the end of his life. It was through this notice that his best friend, Frank Belknap Long, learned of Lovecraft's passing.

One of those most affected by Lovecraft's death was August Derleth, who, although he had never met Lovecraft, had corresponded regularly with him for more than a decade. Derleth was determined to rescue Lovecraft's stories from the oblivion of the pulp magazines. Shortly before his death Lovecraft had somewhat casually given Derleth permission to market his work to book publishers, and Derleth took this advice to heart. But he had to work, at least initially, with R. H. Barlow, whom Lovecraft had named his literary executor. Barlow came from Kansas City to Providence to help Annie Gamwell sort through Lovecraft's papers. It was Barlow who, over the course of years, persuaded the John Hay Library of Brown University to accept the bulk of Lovecraft's manuscripts and other effects. The library was initially not enthusiastic about accepting the papers of an obscure pulp writer, but Barlow's insistence persuaded the library that Lovecraft was at least a local author of some minimal importance.

At first, Derleth worked with Barlow in seeking out book publishers for Lovecraft's tales. Derleth initially approached his own publisher, Charles Scribner's Sons, with an immense manuscript of Lovecraft's tales, more than half a million words in length, which he called *The Outsider and Others*. Scribner's, although impressed with Lovecraft's work, was hesitant to issue so large a volume by an otherwise unrecognized author.

At this point Derleth made a strategic decision: he would publish the book himself. It is clear from his own account that Scribner's would have accepted a smaller book of Lovecraft's stories, but Derleth was fixated on publishing *The Outsider and Others* as he had initially compiled it. So he teamed up with fellow midwesterner Donald Wandrei to establish Arkham House. The book duly came out in 1939.

It made a bit of a splash, but perhaps more as a testimonial to friendship than for its intrinsic merits. Reviews were generally polite, especially a brief but enthusiastic one from Thomas O. Mabbott, a leading Poe scholar. Derleth proceeded with other books by Arkham House—

not only by Lovecraft (*Beyond the Wall of Sleep*, 1943; *Marginalia*, 1944), but by other weird writers, including himself. In this way, Arkham House quickly became the leading small press in the horror field. At the same time, however, it furthered the ghettoization of weird fiction, which continued to be a pariah in the world of mainstream publishing.

Lovecraft's reputation was bolstered by the publication of a selection, *Best Supernatural Stories of H. P. Lovecraft* (1945), by the World Publishing Company. But he received a posthumous body blow when Edmund Wilson, a leading American critic and reviewer, slammed Lovecraft in the review-article "Tales of the Marvellous and the Ridiculous" (*New Yorker*, November 24, 1945). Wilson condemned Lovecraft in no uncertain terms: "The only real horror of these fictions is the horror of bad taste and bad art." Wilson had a serious prejudice against genre fiction (he had attacked Agatha Christie and J. R. R. Tolkien in earlier articles), and he clearly held Lovecraft's association with the pulp magazines against him.

And yet, Lovecraft would not go away. Derleth continued to promote his friend and mentor wherever he could, but he did so in ways that were not always

ABOVE: *August Derleth at work in his office at Arkham House, the independent publishing company he founded in 1939 with Donald Wandrei to release the work of H. P. Lovecraft and other like-minded writers.*

THE MYTHOS GROWS

productive. In particular, he developed something of an obsession with Lovecraft's pseudomythology, which he labeled the Cthulhu Mythos. Not only did he write tale after tale about the Mythos, in such volumes as *The Mask of Cthulhu* (1958) and *The Trail of Cthulhu* (1962), but he also wrote what he called "posthumous collaborations" with Lovecraft, taking story ideas from Lovecraft's "commonplace book" (a collection of plot germs that he had been keeping since at least 1920) and writing unimaginative narratives based on them.

Derleth seriously misconstrued the basic thrust of Lovecraft's myth cycle, believing, among other things, that the "gods" of the Mythos really were gods, and in fact were elementals (symbols for the four elements—earth, air, fire, and water—of medieval philosophy). In particular, Derleth, a devout Catholic, claimed that Lovecraft's Mythos was fundamentally similar to Christianity. He could make this argument because he himself invented, out of whole cloth, a series of benign entities, the Elder Gods, who fought on the side of humanity against the "evil" Old Ones like Cthulhu and Yog-Sothoth. Derleth's misconceptions of the Mythos hindered the proper understanding of Lovecraft and his work for decades.

The 1950s were a lean period for weird fiction in general and Lovecraft in particular. The demise of the pulp magazines (*Weird Tales* folded in 1954) coincided with the emergence of the paperback book, but weird fiction did not flourish in this new format. Those writers who wished to write horror and supernatural fiction had to do so under the guise of writing science fiction or suspense fiction. Robert Bloch became famous in this period, writing *Psycho* (1959) and other suspense novels; Fritz Leiber wrote *Conjure Wife* (1943) and other tales that fused horror and science fiction. But this was also the heyday of writers such as Ray Bradbury, Richard Matheson, and Charles Beaumont, who rebelled against Lovecraft's dense prose style and his emphasis on cosmicism, focusing instead on horrors that emerged from the realms of everyday life.

The tide began to turn in the 1960s, when the first film adaptations of Lovecraft's work appeared. His tales had been adapted for radio shows such as *Suspense* from as early as 1949, but the films *The Haunted Palace* (1963), directed by Roger Corman, and *Die, Monster, Die!* (1965),

RIGHT: *A poster for the first full-length film based on a Lovecraft story,* The Haunted Palace, *1963. It was inspired by* The Case of Charles Dexter Ward.

THE MYTHOS GROWS

directed by Daniel Haller, attracted much greater notice. The first was an adaptation of *The Case of Charles Dexter Ward*, with a screenplay by Charles Beaumont and starring Vincent Price, but Lovecraft's relative obscurity caused the studio to release the film as part of Corman's Poe series ("The Haunted Palace" is a poem inserted into "The Fall of the House of Usher"). *Die, Monster, Die!* is an adaptation of "The Colour out of Space," featuring Boris Karloff. Neither film ranks particularly high as an artistic product, but they did help to bring Lovecraft's name to a wider audience. A third film, *The Shuttered Room* (1967), is an adaptation of a Lovecraft-Derleth "posthumous collaboration," but the Lovecraft content is minimal.

The rights to these films were sold by Derleth, and the revenues engendered by them allowed him to reprint Lovecraft's fiction in three volumes in 1963–65. He also issued the first volume of Lovecraft's *Selected Letters* (1965), an enormously important series (eventually published in five volumes) that would lead to a revolution in our understanding of Lovecraft the man and writer.

The momentum from all these ventures now seemed inexorable. Lovecraft's work appeared in two widely distributed paperback editions from Lancer Books, setting the stage for the so-called Arkham Edition of H. P. Lovecraft, published first by Beagle Books and later by Ballantine Books (a division of Random House) beginning in 1969. This was the first time that Lovecraft's work had appeared in mass-market paperbacks from a major publisher, and the result was instantaneous. The books cumulatively sold millions of copies over the next few years, prompting *Time* magazine to publish a review by Philip Herrera ("The Dream Lurker," June 11, 1973) that affectionately parodied Lovecraft's flamboyant style but emphasized the unexpected popularity of his work.

It was at this time, also, that a new scholarly interest in Lovecraft began to emerge. Lovecraft criticism—if it can be called that—had been appearing in fanzines since the time of Lovecraft's death, but its influence was all but invisible, given that August Derleth was regarded by the general literary world as Lovecraft's preeminent interpreter. It was only Derleth's death on July 4, 1971, that allowed other views to emerge. At that time, Lovecraft scholarship was led by Dirk W. Mosig, a German-born professor of psychology who questioned many aspects of Derleth's understanding of Lovecraft, especially his views of the Cthulhu Mythos. Mosig and others began the herculean task of overturning Derleth's tendentious interpretations and revealing Lovecraft as the powerful writer and keen thinker that he was.

In 1975, a trio of books appeared: L. Sprague de Camp's *Lovecraft: A Biography*, the first full-length biography of the author; Frank Belknap Long's *Howard Phillips Lovecraft: Dreamer on the Nightside*, a somewhat uneven memoir; and Willis Conover's *Lovecraft at Last*, an exquisitely produced book by one who, as a teenager, had known Lovecraft for the last six months of the latter's life. De Camp's biography, published by Doubleday, was widely distributed, but it was criticized for its unsympathetic view of Lovecraft and its harping on Lovecraft's racism; Long's memoir, in fact, was written as an attempted rebuttal to de Camp's book, much of which Long had read in manuscript.

LEFT: *A still from the second Lovecraft film,* Die, Monster, Die! *(1965), which was based on* The Colour Out of Space.

These developments in Lovecraft scholarship occurred in the context of the sudden and unexpected emergence of horror fiction as a best-selling phenomenon. Spurred by the popularity of such novels as Ira Levin's *Rosemary's Baby* (1967), Thomas Tryon's *The Other* (1971), and William Peter Blatty's *The Exorcist* (1971)—and, more pertinently, by the immensely successful film adaptations of these books—horror fiction began to dominate the best-seller lists, and such writers as Stephen King, Peter Straub, Clive Barker, and Anne Rice became household names.

As a result, earlier works of horror fiction began to be reprinted, especially in the landmark Ballantine Adult Fantasy Series, edited by Lin Carter. Readers of horror fiction, unlike the majority of science fiction or mystery readers, have always been interested in reading the classics of the field; Lovecraft benefited from this tendency, even though few of the new popular horror writers looked to him as a model. King, in his nonfiction book *Danse Macabre* (1981), did refer to Lovecraft flamboyantly as "the twentieth-century horror story's dark and baroque prince," but his own work—with the exception of the Cthulhu Mythos novelette "Jerusalem's Lot" (1978)—was antipodal to Lovecraft's richly textured prose, slow-moving action, and absence of distinctive characters. Instead, King and others followed the tradition of Bradbury and Matheson in setting their novels and tales in the mundane world of suburbia, with horror emerging from the humdrum life of people going to work, having families, and struggling with the commonplace issues that people everywhere face.

But horror's popularity couldn't help but raise Lovecraft in the esteem of at least a certain devoted core of aficionados. A notable band of genuine literary artists also emerged in the 1970s and 1980s, and although they attracted far less attention than the best sellers, they not only produced outstanding horror fiction but also highlighted their connections with Lovecraft and other classic authors.

British writer Ramsey Campbell had his first volume—a collection of Lovecraft pastiches entitled *The Inhabitant of the Lake and Less Welcome Tenants*—published by Arkham House in 1964, when he was eighteen. He went on to write some of the most distinguished supernatural fiction of the next several decades. Although few of his works were directly influenced by Lovecraft, his novels and tales repeatedly harked back to the Providence writer for their inspiration.

> "READERS OF HORROR FICTION . . . HAVE ALWAYS BEEN INTERESTED IN READING THE CLASSICS OF THE FIELD."

Two American writers who were partial disciples of Campbell continued the trend. T. E. D. Klein, in the novel *The Ceremonies* (1984) and the story collection *Dark Gods* (1985), adapted the Lovecraft idiom to the bustle and clangor of present-day New York City. Klein had gone to Brown and written an honors thesis on Lovecraft and Lord Dunsany, so his knowledge ran deep. Thomas Ligotti is remarkable for developing an underground reputation with such story collections as *Songs of a Dead Dreamer* (1986) and *Grimscribe* (1991), in which he adapted Lovecraft to his distinctively bizarre and nightmarish vision.

It was at this time that thousands of textual errors were discovered in the standard Arkham House editions of Lovecraft's work. The three Arkham House volumes of Lovecraft fiction from the 1960s had been kept in print; the new corrected editions emerged in the mid-1980s. Readers were thrilled to read Lovecraft's tales as they were originally written, without the errors introduced by his editors.

Scholarship on Lovecraft continued, chiefly in the journal *Lovecraft Studies*. This work culminated in the H. P. Lovecraft Centennial Conference at Brown University in 1990, which brought in scholars from around the world to discuss a wide array of subjects relating to Lovecraft. At the conclusion of the Centennial Conference, a plaque commemorating Lovecraft's birth was erected at the John Hay Library of Brown University—the first time that Providence recognized the contributions of one of its most celebrated native sons.

Published scholarship flourished at this time, with important new critical studies by Peter Cannon, Donald R. Burleson, the Finnish scholar Timo Airaksenen, and others. A few years later I wrote a lengthy biography, *H. P. Lovecraft: A Life* (1996).

Penguin Classics published three annotated volumes based on corrected texts of Lovecraft's work between 1999 and 2004. For the first time in his posthumous existence, Lovecraft was marketed as "literature" rather than as a genre writer. These volumes led to Peter Straub's edition of Lovecraft's *Tales*, published in 2005 by the Library of America. Exactly sixty years after being dismissed by Edmund Wilson as the epitome of "bad taste and bad art," Lovecraft entered the definitive canon of American literature. The book was a critical and commercial success—something that never could have been said about Lovecraft during his lifetime.

The remarkable thing about Lovecraft is his continuing popular appeal. Comic-book adaptations of Lovecraft's stories have been appearing since the 1950s but became particularly numerous from the 1970s onward. Such well-known artists as Richard Corben, Ron Goulart, and John Coulthart have adapted many of Lovecraft's tales for such comics as *Skull* and *Creepy*, and several publishers have now issued book-length graphic novels including adaptations of Lovecraft's stories as well as original stories where Lovecraft is featured as a character.

Lovecraft has been a popular figure with rock bands also. His influence on psychedelic rock, heavy metal, and punk is extensive. In the 1960s there was even a band called H. P. Lovecraft, which issued two albums. Such bands as Metallica, Black Sabbath, Blue Öyster Cult, and the Mountain Goats include allusions to Lovecraftian elements in their music.

Film and television adaptations have also been numerous. Rod Serling adapted "Cool Air" and "Pickman's Model" in 1971 episodes of his television anthology series *Night Gallery*. A film, *The Dunwich Horror* (1970), implausibly starred the handsome Dean Stockwell as Wilbur Whateley and featured a newly introduced character

ABOVE: *A still from* The Dunwich Horror, *starring Dean Stockwell and Sandra Dee, 1970.*

Henry Wheeler strained his eye at the telescope, but saw only the three grotesquely silhouetted human figures on the peak, all moving their arms furiously in strange gestures as their incantation drew near its culmination. From what black wells of Acherontic fear or feeling, from what unplumbed gulfs of extra-cosmic consciousness or obscure, long-latent heredity, were those half-articulate thunder-croakings drawn? Presently they began to gather renewed force and coherence as they grew in stark, utter, ultimate frenzy.

–"THE DUNWICH HORROR,"
H. P. LOVECRAFT

played by Sandra Dee. (Even though the Old Ones were depicted as drug-crazed hippies, the film had its moments.)

In 1982, the California gaming company Chaosium issued a role-playing game, The Call of Cthulhu, that was immediately popular and continues to be so up to the present day. This game took a generously catholic view of the Cthulhu Mythos, including the "gods," books, and other entities created by other writers alongside those invented by Lovecraft; but more importantly, it led many players of the game to read Lovecraft's stories for the first time.

In 1985, the film *H. P. Lovecraft's Re-animator*, directed by Stuart Gordon, was released. A campy, over-the-top adaptation of "Herbert West–Reanimator," it featured an engaging, manic performance by Jeffrey Combs as Herbert West. The film was weirdly faithful to certain aspects of the story, especially given that the tale itself was very likely a self-parody. Gordon followed up this film with *From Beyond* (1986), while his colleague Brian Yuzna directed the hilarious *Bride of Re-animator* (1990). These successful horror films induced other independent filmmakers to try their hand at Lovecraft adaptations.

Meanwhile, a cadre of newer writers of horror fiction had absorbed the findings of the past several decades of Lovecraft scholarship and approached the Cthulhu Mythos with a firmer understanding of the essence of Lovecraft's cosmic vision. The richly complex tales of Caitlin R. Kiernan and Laird Barron are infused with Lovecraftian elements. Donald Tyson wrote a fascinating historical-supernatural novel, *Alhazred* (2006), about the author of the *Necronomicon*. Noted Lovecraft scholar Peter Cannon, in *The Lovecraft Chronicles* (2004), was one of several writers who used Lovecraft himself as a fictional character. Michael Shea's *Copping Squid* (2009), Brian Stableford's *The Womb of Time* (2010), and Rick Dakan's *Cthulhu Cult* (2011) are only three of the more interesting treatments of the Cthulhu Mythos to emerge in recent years. Anthologists were not slow in following suit, collecting new Mythos-related fiction. Stephen Jones edited the notable anthology *Shadows Over Innsmouth* (1994), in which contemporary writers includ-

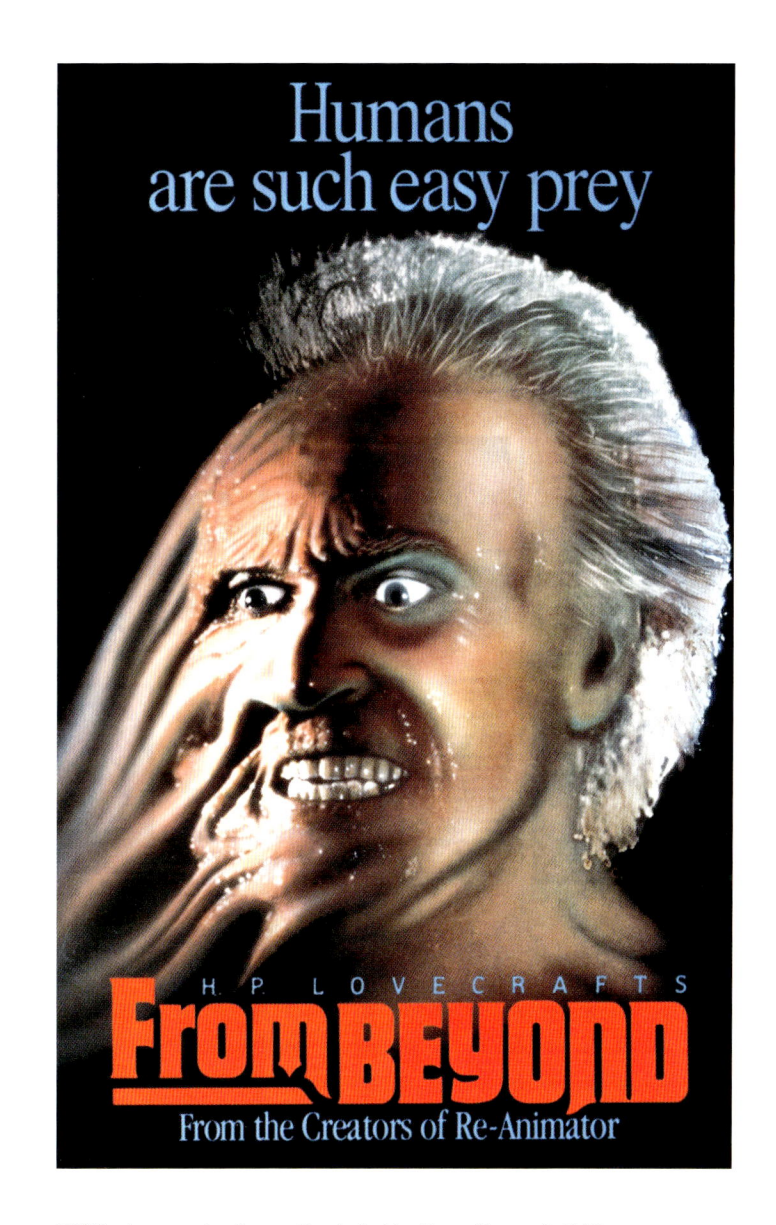

ABOVE: *A poster for Stuart Gordon's film* From Beyond, *1986.*

LEFT: *Jeffrey Combs as Herbert West in Stuart Gordon's* Bride of Re-Animator, *1990.*

THE MYTHOS GROWS

ABOVE: *H. P. Lovecraft in 1934, another of the Lucius Truesdell photographs.*

ing Neil Gaiman and Ramsey Campbell wrote imaginative takeoffs of "The Shadow Over Innsmouth."

The breadth of interest in Lovecraft, from gawky teenagers to highbrow literary artists, continues to amaze. Consider the case of Jorge Luis Borges. As early as 1967, this distinguished Argentinian writer had included a discussion of Lovecraft in his slim treatise, *Introducción a la literatura norteamericana* (translated into English as An *Introduction to American Literature*, 1971). He then wrote a sensitive story, "There Are More Things" (*Atlantic Monthly*, July 1975), dedicated "To the memory of H. P. Lovecraft." Borges's appreciation of Lovecraft was, however, not unmixed: when he reprinted "There Are More Things" in *The Book of Sand*, he referred to Lovecraft as "an unconscious parodist of Poe"!

Writers ranging from S. J. Perelman, Woody Allen, Gore Vidal, Paul Theroux, and Umberto Eco have included references to, or discussions of, Lovecraft in their various works. In his memoir, *Palimpsest* (1995), Vidal refers in passing to a classmate who let out a scream in school: "It was a cry from another species or world. An H. P. Lovecraft ghoul's eldritch howl or the blast Tarzan's Tantor the Elephant made." Vidal clearly expects every reader to understand the allusion.

Lovecraft's worldwide reputation is now assured. He has been translated into more than twenty-five languages, from Catalan to Serbo-Croatian, from Romanian to Turkish, from Bengali to modern Greek. Lovecraft's reputation in France is so eminent that, as early as 1969, the prestigious literary magazine *L'Herne* devoted an entire issue to him, and doctoral dissertations in French, Italian, and other European languages appear with regularity. The highly acclaimed writer Michel Houellebecq wrote a lively treatise, *H. P. Lovecraft: Contre le monde, contre la vie* (1991), which was quickly translated into English, German, Italian, and Spanish.

His status as a pop-culture figure continues to grow right alongside his literary reputation. Lovecraftian merchandising has taken off; plush Cthulhu dolls make popular gifts along with jewelry based on his outlandish entities. Film adaptations, short and long, have grown almost too numerous to chart. The independent film industry is so taken with Lovecraft that an annual H. P. Lovecraft Film Festival is held in Portland, Oregon.

And yet, Lovecraft continues to benefit from the fact that his reputation is not entirely respectable. Fans have always had a sense that he is not and never will be fully part of the literary mainstream, and his status as a cult figure who occasionally attracts some dubious followers–from the Satanist Anton LaVey to the eccentric Robert Anton Wilson, author of the *Illuminatus!* trilogy–has much to do with his continuing appeal. Devotees of goth culture draw inspiration from Lovecraft and his monsters, and occultists like Kenneth Grant have created a cottage industry in claiming that creatures like Cthulhu and Yog-Sothoth actually exist in the remote corners of the cosmos.

That Lovecraft will continue to be read for generations by a wide and variegated readership seems clear. His uniquely nightmarish vision of a fragile humanity lost in the incalculable vortices of space and time, expressed in prose that is rich, dense, and evocative, seems to resonate over the generations. While so many writers of the past have dated themselves by focusing on transient social concerns, Lovecraft conveyed the existential angst of human beings who find themselves simultaneously attracted and terrified by the vastness of the cosmos. The gaunt, lantern-jawed dreamer from Providence has become part of his own mythology, and he continues in spirit to stalk the streets of his native city and any other place where people turn to face the abyss–and find it looking back at them.

AUTHOR BIOGRAPHY

S. T. JOSHI is the author of such critical studies as *The Weird Tale* (1990), *H. P. Lovecraft: The Decline of the West* (1990), and *Unutterable Horror: A History of Supernatural Fiction* (2012). He has prepared corrected editions of H. P. Lovecraft's work and annotated editions of the weird tales of Lovecraft, Algernon Blackwood, Lord Dunsany, M. R. James, and Arthur Machen, as well as the anthology *American Supernatural Tales* (2007).

Joshi's exhaustive biography, *H. P. Lovecraft: A Life* (1996), won the British Fantasy Award and the Bram Stoker Award from the Horror Writers Association; an unabridged and updated edition has appeared as *I Am Providence: The Life and Times of H. P. Lovecraft* (2010). He has also edited works by Ambrose Bierce, H. L. Mencken, and other writers, and has written on religion, politics, and race relations.

IMAGE CREDITS

Cover: Bill Whitaker and Mind the Mix/Veer
Page 7: Everett Collection
Page 8: The Library of Congress
Page 11: Private Collection/The Bridgeman Art Library and Dover Publications
Page 14: NASA
Page 16: John Hay Library, Brown University Library
Page 18: The Library of Congress
Page 19: John Hay Library, Brown University Library
Page 20: John Hay Library, Brown University Library
Page 21: akg-images
Page 23: FPG/Getty Images
Page 25: John Hay Library, Brown University Library
Page 26: Central Saint Martins College of Art and Design, London/The Bridgeman Art Library
Page 28: English School/Getty Images
Page 32: NASA and Ricardo Chahad/stock.xchng
Page 35: Courtesy of S. T. Joshi
Page 36: John Hay Library, Brown University Library
Page 38: SuperStock/Getty Images
Page 40: Isy Ochoa/Getty Images
Page 43: Bettmann/Corbis
Page 44: John Hay Library, Brown University Library
Page 45: John Hay Library, Brown University Library
Page 46: Courtesy of S. T. Joshi
Page 48: Advertising Archive/Courtesy Everett Collection
Page 50: Bill Whitaker
Page 53: John Hay Library, Brown University Library
Page 57: Barbara Singer/Getty Images
Page 61: The Library of Congress
Page 63: John Hay Library, Brown University Library
Page 65: John Hay Library, Brown University Library
Page 67: John Hay Library, Brown University Library
Page 68: The Library of Congress
Page 70: Time & Life Pictures/Getty Images
Page 72: Courtesy of Terence McVicker
Page 74: Advertising Archive/Courtesy Everett Collection
Page 76: Getty Images
Page 78: NASA and Library of Congress

Page 81: Courtesy of S. T. Joshi
Page 83: The Library of Congress
Page 84: APIC/Getty Images
Page 86: John Hay Library, Brown University Library
Page 90: Bettmann/Corbis
Page 94: Corbis and NASA
Page 97: John Hay Library, Brown University Library
Page 101: John Hay Library, Brown University Library
Page 105: SuperStock/Getty Images
Page 107: John Hay Library, Brown University Library
Page 109: Getty Images
Page 112: The Library of Congress
Page 114: John Hay Library, Brown University Library
Page 117: Getty Images
Page 119: John Hay Library, Brown University Library
Page 120: Lars Sundstrom/stock.xchng
Page 123: The Granger Collection
Page 125: John Hay Library, Brown University Library
Page 126: John Hay Library, Brown University Library
Page 128: John Hay Library, Brown University Library
Page 132: Mary Evans Picture Library/Everett Collection
Page 135: John Hay Library, Brown University Library
Page 137: John Hay Library, Brown University Library
Page 138: The Library of Congress
Page 140: Courtesy of S. T. Joshi
Page 141: John Hay Library, Brown University Library
Page 142: NASA
Page 145: Courtesy of the August Derleth Society
Page 147: Mary Evans/AIP/Ronald Grant/Everett Collection
Page 148: Everett Collection
Page 153: Everett Collection
Page 154: Everett Collection
Page 155: Mary Evans/Ronald Grant/Everett Collection
Page 156: John Hay Library, Brown University Library
Page 158: dmvphotos/Shutterstock
Back cover: NASA

Photographs and other illustrations used by permission of Lovecraft Holdings, LLC.